Andy

GREEK PHILOSOPHERS

CONSTANTINE PLEVRIS

GREEK PHILOSOPHERS

EFSTATHIADIS GROUP

EFSTATHIADIS GROUP S.A.
14, Valtetsiou Str.
106 80 Athens
Tel: (01) 5154650, 6450113
Fax: (01) 5154657
GREECE

ISBN 960 226 537 X

Printed and bound in Greece

TABLE OF CONTENTS

PROLOGUE

The term "philosophy" is Greek. It is a compound formed from the words philos, meaning "friend," and sophia meaning "sapience," "wisdom." Thus, a philosopher is one who loves wisdom, that is, complete true knowledge.

According to Plato (Phaedrus, 278D) only God is in full possession of wisdom. Man, finding himself between knowledge and ignorance, desires to attain complete true knowledge and struggles to do so. So, man is not wise because he does not possess wisdom as God does; however, man is a philosopher, (meaning he is) a lover of wisdom, and aspires after it. God is wise, man is a lover of wisdom.

The word philosophy is first encountered in Heraclitus (35); there he maintains that "it is necessary for those who are philosophers to have investigated very many things"(χρή γάρ εὖ μάλα πολλά φιλοσόφους ἄνδρας εἶναι). Nevertheless, there also exists the point of view that Pythagoras was the first to call himself a philosopher. According to Diogenes Laertius (48,8) when Leon the Tyrant of Phlius asked Pythagoras, "What are you?"(τίς εἴη;) he answered, "A philosopher" (φιλόσοφος εἰπεῖν).

The word "philosophy" itself contains the essence of philosophy which is the discovery of complete truth.

Philosophy is undoubtedly a Greek creation. Greece is the sole mother of philosophy. During ancient times, when other peoples had prophets, moralists, religious leaders, and gods, the Greeks had philosophers. In his book What Philosophy Is M. Heidegger frankly admits that ".Philosophy is Greek in its existence....". Philosophy in its original existence is of such a nature that only the Greek world could have conceived of it first. E. Zeller and W. Nestle in their monumental work, Grundiss der Geschichte der Griechischen Philosophie, say, "Greek philosophy, like all the products of the Greek mind, is characteristically effortless and basic to the development of the whole of the civilisation of Western Europe. The Greeks posed the fundamental questions of theoretical and practical philosophy and answered them with the usual Greek clarity. They developed the basic concepts of philosophy and, as physics and philosophy were one, also developed a large portion/a major part/portion of the concepts of the science of physics. It is through and within these concepts that latter day European science and philosophy move. Greek philosophy became the mother of all European philosophy. The philosophical ideas which we find in the works of the Romans are not original; they are taken from the Greeks and transferred to the Medieval and Modern world in their Latin garment.

Will Durant, too, supports these beliefs. In his World History of Civilisation he says that "Greece (through the Romans) bequeathed her sciences, philosophy, and arts and letters to Europe. These are the cornerstone of the civilisation of the modern world. Except for machinery there is almost nothing eternal in our civilisation which does not come from Greece ". Even Fr. Engels in his Dialectics of Nature recognizes that in philosophy, as well as in other areas, we are constantly obliged to return to the accomplishments of this small people (the Greeks). Their multifaceted/various talents (χαρίσματα) and efficiency/activities assured this race of such a place in the history of mankind as no other.

This book is a brief survey of the fundamental schools of philosophy of Ancient Greece. We are trying to give the reader a picture of the ideas the Ancient Greeks proclaimed. We are also introducing the main representatives of these schools of thought. We hope that in this we are doing a service to those who have not sufficient time/time enough or the inclination to study Ancient Greek philosophy yet want to have a taste of it.

IONIAN SCHOOL

THALES OF MILETUS

Thales of Miletus (624-546 B.C.)

Thales is generally considered the first Greek philosopher and scientist. Thus he may be called the founder of philosophy and science for mankind. Born in Miletus, he nevertheless was of Boeotian ancestry. In fact, according to the renowned historian and tyrant of Samos, Douris, (Δοῦρις -ιδος) Thales descended from the family of the Thelides, who where descendants of Cadmus, the national hero of the Thebans. On the other hand, Herodotus (I, 170) evidently misled by Thales' father's foreign name (Examnyus) considers Thales' most distant ancestry to have been Phoenician ("τό ἀνέκαθεν γένος ἐόντος Φοίνικος") (I, 170). However, this belief is mistaken for two reasons besides Douris' evidence. First, because Thales was actively involved in the public affairs of his home town, an activity which he would have been forbidden if he had been a barbarian. The main reason, however is that the dependable biographer Hermippus preserved the following fact: that Thales used to say that he was grateful to Fate for three reasons. These reasons were: first, that he was born a human being and not an animal; secondly, that he was born a man and not a woman; and finally that he has born a Greek and not a barbarian.(" Ἔφασκε γάρ τριῶν τούτων ἕνεκα χάριν ἔχειν τῆς τύχης· πρῶτον μέν ὅτι ἄνθρωπος ἐγενόμην καί οὐ θηρίον· εἶτα δέ ἀνήρ καί οὐ γυνή καί τρίτον Ἕλλην καί οὐ βάρβαρος "). Refer to Diogenes Laertius (I, 32) as regards this matter although there is no reason for this since now no one doubts Thales' Greek heritage.

Thales took advantage of the opportunity which Miletus offered him as the junction of trade routes and travelled to Egypt and Persia. In Egypt he managed to determine the height of the Pyramids by means of the shadows they cast and gave his own interpretation to the flooding of the Nile. He attributed the floods to the fact that the river currents are checked by strong winds which blow against their flow. He most certainly received much information from the Egyptian priests but, as evidenced by many ancient texts, he taught them at the same time.

His success in the area of science was of unprecedented significance, especially in geometry. In this field he discovered and mathematically proved: a) that the two base angles of an isosceles triangle are equal; b) that the diameter bisects a circle; and c) that given the base and the angles of 2 sides we can construct a triangle. Besides, as Plutarch states, Thales understood the properties of like triangles and even proved that the angle inscribed in a semicircle is a right angle.

Thales also made significant discoveries in astronomy. Naturally, the most impressive was the prediction of the solar eclipse which took place on 28 May 585 B.C. (by the Julian calendar). This was the world's first such prediction and Thales was led to it through his study of the orbits of the sun and moon; when the orbits coincided vertically an eclipse resulted. Aetius gives us Thales' theory as follows: " Θαλῆς πρῶτος ἔφη ἐκλείπειν τόν Ἥλιον τῆς Σελήνης αὐτόν ὑπερχομένης κατά κάθετον ".

It is equally important to bear in mind Thales' discoveries as regards Ursa Minor, the discovery of true North, his investigations regarding the measuring of the diameter of the sun and moon in relation to their apparent orbits, a means to measure space in order to calculate how far from land ships are, etc.

Thales' practical applications of his theories are as

exceptional as his theoretical innovations. One such practical application was the re-routing of the Halyus River by means of a canal so that the troops of King Croesus of Lydia could cross it. Thales was, in a way, King Croesus' technical advisor. Thales deserves much credit because he was the first to note the phenomena of magnetism and electricity so that he should, in fact, be considered the discoverer of electricity. He observed the power of electricity in amber, a type of fossilized resin which can attract various particles through friction.

Thales' basic contribution to philosophy and science is his establishing the principle of the theoretical quest for the cause of phenomena on which principle all philosophical and scientific thought is based. Thus the theoretical definition of the cause, which provides the explanation for the phenomena, takes the place of random experimentation.

Philosophically Thales is a monist; that is to say, he believes that the basic substance of all being is one: water "Ἀρχήν δέ τῶν πάντων ὕδωρ ὑπεστήσατο"(Diogenes Laertius, I, 27). Everything we see comes from water and constitutes a simple change of this single substance of all beings. However, this basic substance, water, and everything that comes from it is not dead. They are full of life, full of energy. It is therefore a mistake to classify Thales as a materialist because even though he accepted one material (water) as the basic substance of being, the material was not lifeless. It was brimming with energy. All beings originate from water and these beings, as does water itself, exist in an unbreakable bond with a dynamic force which is the counterpart of the animated by a force which is found within them in place of a soul"τόν λίθον, ἔφη, ψυχήν ἔχειν " (Ibid).

Since Thales considered matter to be alive we can

maintain that he is the founder of the philosophy which made its appearance much later under the name of hylozoism or hylopsychism and which holds that every material object has a soul whether it self-existently is its own or provided by the soul of the world.

Thales political beliefs were undisputably anti-democratic in the sense that he did not accept the argument that all men are equal. He supported racial discrimination between Greeks and non-Greeks (barbarians) and was unguardedly in favour of national unity and the centralization of the government.

Before their downfall as Herodotus says, the Ionians could have benefited from Thales advice. As political advisor, Thales had recommended that they close the councils (boule) of the various states and establish one on the island of Teon which was located in the centre of Ionia (" Χρηστή δέ καί πρίν ή διαφθαρῆναι Ἰωνίων Θαλέω ἀνδρός Μιλησίου [γνώμη] ἐγένετο ὅς ἐκέλευε ἕν βουλευτήριον Ἴωνας ἐκτῆσθαι ").He also turned against the holders of capital of the time, preaching that no one should make money in an immoral way.(" Μή πλούτει κακώς "). He believed in God, who, according to his beliefs, was the most ancient of beings with respect to age because his God was unborn. (" Πρεσβύτατον τῶν ὄντων Θεός· ἀγέννητον γάρ ").

Very little is known to us about Thales' private life. That human soul ("καί ἐν τῷ ὅλῳ δέ τινες αὐτήν [τήν ψυχήν] μεμῖχθαι φασίν..." Aristotle, Psychology I, 5). For example, just as the human body has the soul, so are all material beings which we know for sure is that he was highly esteemed by the Greeks, who placed him among the seven wise men. The following anecdote has been handed down to us. When his mother tried to pressure him to get married when he was young he would reply " οὔπω καιρός" (that is, the time has not yet come). When he grew older his response to her insistence would be, " οὐκέτι καιρός" (that is, the time [for marriage] is now past).

Finally, it may be concluded from his sayings that Thales was of a superior moral character. Once, when he was asked how we can live justly and well he answered, "By not doing things which we disapprove of in others. (" Ἐάν ἅ τοῖς ἄλλοις ἐπιτιμῶμεν αὐτά μή δρῶμεν "). This moral axiom of behaviour was transferred to the Bible with the phrase “Do unto others as you would have them do unto you ”.

Anaximander (611-546 B.C.)

Anaximander was born in Miletus and was a pupil (i.e. auditor) of Thales. It seems that he was born of a noble family as they headed a "colonizing party" to the Black Sea. Very little is known of his private life. We know that his father's name was Praxiade, that he was a magnificent dresser, that he went to Sparta where he settled various matters concerning the calendar and other minor details.

Anaximander was the first to publish a book, De Naturae in which the Cosmos/universe was given a scientific interpretation, excluding any mythology or illusions. Evidently Aristotle had studied this book even though it was difficult to find. Only a small fragment has reached us. Nevertheless, this fragment is sufficient evidence for us to conclude that the Miletian philosopher wrote in a poetic style with a considerably forceful turn of phrase.

Anaximander was also the first to make a map of the world. " Πρῶτος ἐτόλμησε τήν οἰκουμένην ἐν πίνακι γράψαι" as the ancient geographer, Agathemerus, observed. The Ionian seamen had, of course, worked out maps for themselves but they were not based on scientific data as was Anaximander's, which was sketched geometrically, nor did they represent all of the earth. The seamen's maps represented only portions of it.

Devoting himself to astronomy, Anaximander managed to do a number of wonderful things. For example, he made up a rule by which he determined the equinoxes. He also measured the distance between the stars and placed them in the firmament as well. His observation (which has recently been supported) that there is not only one Cosmos but many, is worthy of mention. However, it is Anaximander's theory as to the origin of life that is most astonishing. It gives rise to many serious thoughts even to this day.

After rejecting the mythological explanation of the origin of the universe and beings, Anaximander accepted a space in which there is perpetual motion as the origin of beings. (He was also the originator of the concept of origin.) He taught that the Cosmos was not created through a change in a primary substance (e.g. water as Thales claimed) but rather through the emanation of opposites (i.e. opposing forms of matter) after the action of perpetual motion. " Οὗτος δέ οὐκ ἀλλοιουμένου τοῦ στοιχείου τήν γένεσιν ποιεῖν, ἀλλ'ἀποκρινομένων τῶν ἐναντίων διά τῆς ἀϊδίου κινήσεως". (Simplicius).

In other words, the universe had its origins in perpetual motion from whose emanations a substance capable of producing heat was born; "φησί δέ τό εἰς τοῦ ἀϊδίου γόνιμον θερμοῦ τε καί ψυχροῦ κατά τήν γένεσιν τοῦδε τοῦ κόσμου ἀποκριθῆναι", as Anaximander's words were handed down to us by the neo-Platonic philosopher Eusebius. The opposition between land and sea, etc. is derived from the opposition of heat and cold.

It would only be reasonable to wonder what Anaximander meant when he maintained that infinity is the origin (πρώτη ἀρχή) of beings. Many different theories have been developed on this subject because, as we have already said, Anaximander's works have not reached us so we do not know his exact views on infinity

In our opinion, however, in using the term "infinity" Anaximander wanted to exclude every known substance as being the origin of beings since, from the moment this substance was known it would cease to be infinite as "infinite" means qualitatively undefined and quantitatively boundless. Infinity also has no bonds in time or space had therefore existed before living beings which are finite. Not having limits it [infinity] can not be perceived by the senses but rather conceived by the mind. Therefore, infinity cannot be not only a known substance but not even matter. (Besides, let us not forget the fact that the definition for substance was given after Aristotle). In addition to this, infinity is eternal because it is unborn and imperishable " ἔτι δέ, καί ἀγέννητον καί ἄφθαρτον".(Mullach, Frag. 1860, page 240). Besides, everything comes from it [infinity] and is governed by it "περιέχειν ἅπαντα καί πάντα κυβερνᾶν".(Ibid). As a result, infinity does not have the same limitations that beings have and, at the same time, thanks to the aforementioned qualities, it goes beyond these things which, like the Cosmos, were created by the perpetual motion of infinity.

Since infinity is not matter but rather (as Aristotle's pupil Theophrastus says) "has another nature which is the opposite of that of substances" ("ἑτέραν φύσιν παρά τά στοιχεῖα"), it is possible to contend that Anaximander most likely considered infinity to be a spirit which emanates the changes of matter through its perpetual motion. Stagiritus' view coincides with this opinion. According to him, one finds in force (it therefore being possible for them to appear) all the substances which later appear through emanation in their origin, that is, in infinity. Whence, according to us, Anaximander's infinity is likened to the absolute spirit, meaning God. This view is supported by the fact that for the ancient Greeks the origin was identical to the divinity. Of course, we infer this from suppositions based on evidence since only a small fragment of Anaximander's work has been preserved, and that thanks to Simplicius. This fragment says " Ἀρχήν τῶν ὄντων τό ἄπειρον · ἐξ ὧν δέ ἡ γένεσις ἐστί τοῖς οὖσι, καί τήν φθοράν εἰς ταῦτα γίνεσθαι καί τό χρεών διδόναι γάρ αὐτά δίκην καί τίσιν ἀλλήλους τῆς ἀδικίας κατά τήν τοῦ χρόνου τάξιν ". This means: The beginning of beings (the substance that is, from which beings arose and which is superior to them) in infinity. Where there is birth in beings there is decay in accordance with inevitable necessity because beings are punished for their imperfection.(In ancient Greek the words " ἄδικον " and " ἄδικία" meant everything which is at a disadvantage). And the one being gives its place to the other as time determines.

According to our interpretation, which is not the only one because Anaximander used words with various interpretations when he wrote, the text, freely interpreted, means that all beings which escaped from infinity took on a form and became finite. As a result they ceased to share in perfection for it exists solely in the origin, meaning infinity. For this reason they are inevitably destroyed, punished precisely because of their imperfection. Once decayed/ destroyed, they no longer have forms or limits and return to infinity.

If we take into consideration the fact that through the above theory Anaximander supported the belief that beings are subject to laws which determine their development, he is certainly the founder of Determinism. But he is not only the founder of Determinism; he is also the founder of the theory of the biological evolution of beings which Darwin later borrowed. As to the evolution of man, the Greek philosopher asserted that when he was first created, man was not as he is today, nor did he originate from human beings as they are today because it takes present-day man many years to reach maturity so that if he had originally been as he is today it would have been impossible for him to survive. So, said

Anaximander, man came into being from another kind of animal. ("Ἐξ αλλοειδέων ζώων ὁ ἄνθρωπος ἐγεννήθη ἐκ τοῦ τά μέν ἄλλα δι' ἑαυτῶν ταχύ νέμεσθαι, μόνον ἀρχάς οὐκ ἄν τότε τοιοῦτον ὄντα διασωθῆναι "). Finally, Anaximander essentially founded the theory of transcendentalism since he was the first to introduce and use infinity as a term transcending beings (life) and not arising from experience.

Anaximenes (585-525 B.C.)

Anaximenes, son of Eurystratus, was a pupil of Anaximander and, as we shall see, gave great progressive impetus to philosophical thought. It is a pity that his work was completely lost so that the little we know of his work has been conveyed to us by other writers through their work.

In the first place we can assert that the last of the Miletian philosophers combined the views of Thales and Anaximander as to the origin of beings. He agreed with Thales that the origin of beings is definite as to quality and agreed with Anaximander that it is boundless as to quantity and contains/embraces perpetual motion. Anaximenes accepted air as the origin of life.

Anaximenes did not come to this realization arbitrarily but after observation. That is, in observing he concluded that air is found everywhere, surrounds everything, and moves and gives life to organisms which die without it. It is also infinite as to quantity. However, there arises the question as to how the various beings were created from air.

Anaximenes did not accept the theory of emanation which Thales introduced. Anaximenes believed that condensation and rarefication are produced here and there through the motion which is inherent to air. These two changes in the equal distribution of air are the causes of the genesis of beings. Therefore, the variety of the forms of life is due to precisely how concentrated or diluted the air is.

More exactly, Anaximenes supported the view that when air is still it lacks characteristics and is, moreover, invisible However, when movement is observed and the equal distribution of its particles disturbed, then air manifests characteristics, i.e. if it is thin it becomes heated and goes on until it turns into fire. On the other hand, if it is dense it becomes liquid and then dry ("τό δέ εἶδος τοῦ ἀέρος τοιοῦτον ὅταν μέν ὁμαλώτατος ᾖ ὄψει ἄδηλον δηλοῦσθαι δέ τῷ ψυχρῷ καί τῷ θερμῷ καί τῷ νοτερῷ καί τῷ κινουμένῳ κινεῖσθαι δέ ἀεί οὐ γάρ μεταβάλλειν ὅσα μεταβάλλει, εἰ μή κινοῖτο. Πυκνούμενον γάρ καί ἀραιούμενον διάφορον φαίνεσθαι· ὅταν γάρ εἰς τό ἀραιότερον διαχυθῇ πῦρ γίνεσθαι, ἀνέμους δέ πάλιν εἶναι ἀέρα πυκνούμενον, ἐξ ἀέρος νέφος ἀποτελεῖσθαι κατά τήν πίλησην, ἔτι δέ μᾶλλον ὕδωρ, ἔτι πλεῖον πυκνωθέντα γῆν καί εἰς τό μάλιστα πυκνότατον λίθους ". Hippolytus). That is, the quality of air is such that when it is in an undisturbed state it cannot be seen, but it appears when it is disturbed, manifesting itself through heat and cold and through humidity and movement since none of these things, which change, would have changed if they had not been in motion. Air appears different when in a dense and when in a rarefied state since, as it diffuses itself it becomes thinner and changes into fire, whereas winds are made up of dense air which, when further condensed, becomes clouds which in turn produce water when further condensed. If we increase the density of the air even more, we get earth and finally, through the greatest condensation, we get stones.

Anaximenes reached these conclusions by means of observation which, in any case, constitutes a scientific method of research since it was done overtly. He checked the results of his observations by means of the following experiment. He pursed his lips and blew onto his hand, upon which he felt cold air which he attributed to the condensation of air caused by the tightening of the lips. Afterwards he blew with his lips wide apart, upon which he felt warm air which he attributed to the thinness of the air. (" Ψύχεται γάρ ἡ πνοή πιεσθεῖσα καί πυκνωθεῖσα τοῖς χείλεσι, ἀνειμένου δέ τοῦ στόματος γίγνεται θερμόν ὑπό μανότητος ". Plutarch, "Περί τοῦ πρώτου ψυχροῦ", 947 E).

Anaximenes' conviction that everything has air as its source (that is, has a common prime substance) but that beings differ among themselves due to differences in the density of the air, grants him the right to be considered the fore-runner of the atomic theory which was later founded by other Greek philosophers. In addition, his belief that the variety of beings due to quantitative changes (denseness-thinness) of the common prime substance (air) renders him the founder of the theory concerning quantitative change due to quantitative accumulation, a theory which Marx formulated (one of the laws of Marxism) thus usurping its authorship.

To finish off, Anaximander considered air to be God. " Τόν ἀέρα Θεόν εἶναι" as has been handed down to us by an ancient writer who collected the views of the philosophical schools. That is all we shall say as to Anaximenes' ontological theories. Now, as to his partial sciences (ἐπιμέρους ἐπιστῆμες) one must mention his contributions to astronomy (in which science he supported the belief that the moon reflects the light of the sun) and mainly to meteorology (in which science he gave correct explanations for the creation of rain, clouds, hail and snow. [" Χάλαζαν δέ γίγνεσθαι ὅταν ἀπό τῶν νεφῶν τό ὕδωρ καταφερόμενον παγῇ. Χιόνα δέ ὅταν αὐτά ἐνυγρότερα ὄντα πῆξιν λάβῃ "]). He also explained how the rainbow is formed. Stephen Halls faithfully copied Anaximenes' views on air. In 1727 in his book entitled Vegetable Statics he wrote, "Air takes part in the composition of bodies wherein it is found in a solid form without its elasticity. Air is the universal link of nature".

PYTHAGOREAN SCHOOL

PYTHAGORAS

Pythagoras (570-496 B.C.)

Pythagoras, of Samian birth, was the son of Mnesarchus and Pythais. The fact that his teaching was exclusively verbal makes it difficult to know his theories exactly. The secrecy which surrounded his teachings contributes to the difficulty. In fact, the secrecy of his teachings was kept by oath. Nevertheless, we have some information from different authors whom we can consider reliable. Thus, Diogenes Laertius, Iamblichus and Porphyrius mention many facts regarding the life and work of the great philosopher.

First of all we should stress the fact that Pythagoras did not found a religious organization, as some people believe, but rather a political club. He headed/was leader of this club until he died, or rather, until he was assassinated by the democrats / exponents/ advocates of democracy under the leadership of Cylon. Only Aechippus, Philolaus, and Lysis were saved from the massacre of the Pythagoreans. Lysis, fleeing to Thebes, became the teacher of Epaminondas.

In his studies Pythagoras used observation as a means of research. Indeed, on observing Nature and ascertaining that order and harmony prevail in it (Nature) he gave the universe the name of Cosmos (the Ancient Greek word for "order") precisely for that reason. In order for this stable order and harmony to exist, however, it is necessary for the existence of beings not to end where our perception of them by the senses ends (phenomena, matter etc.). Obviously there exists a force, a substance, which is inherent to/in all beings, is eternal, is not perceivable by the senses and ensures order and harmony. Pythagoras called this substance Number.

This number naturally, is not mathematical. Although

the term was taken from mathematics, it was not taken as a mathematical term but symbolically in order to indicate the substance which exists in all beings. Taking into consideration that all numbers come from the unit, so beings go back to a common beginning which, symbolically (again), is defined/designated as the unit. For Pythagoras this unit was God without whom neither order nor harmony would rule. Thus Pythagoras recognized the world of numbers as existing parallel to the world of beings. The world of numbers cannot be perceived by the senses; however, it is perceived by the intellect and through indirect contact (intuition).

Pythagoras' world of numbers reminds one of Plato's world of ideas with the difference that Plato considered ideas to be completely separate, whereas Pythagoras believed that numbers were inherent to beings. Aristotle commented on Plato's copying/ reproduction of/ imitation of Pythagorean teaching. In his Metaphysics Aristotle says that Plato took Pythagoras' theory and merely changed the name ("τοὔνομα μεταβαλών") and elsewhere, in his Psychology, he characteristically notes: " οἱ μέν γάρ ἀριθμοί τά εἴδη αὐτά καί ἀρχαί ἐλέγοντο....εἴδη δέ οἱ ἀριθμοί οὔτοι τῶν πραγμάτων". Besides, Plato himself calls ideas numbers at many points of the dialogue "Philebus" (241, 267, 26E).

It was after 2500 years that Pythagoras' theory had justice done to it by science which developed the theory of the atomic number which represents units of energy (electricity) inherent to/in all known forms of matter.

In the area of ethics, Pythagoras believed that, in imitation of the order and harmony of the universe, men should behave in such a way that an analogous order and harmony would exist in their relationships. In order to achieve this it is necessary for virtue to be firstly established in people's consciences. This virtue consists of prudence, justice, and valour. Moreover, friendship had been exalted/glorified by the Pythagoreans to such a degree that when Pythagoras asked himself "What is a friend?" he answered "Another self" (Ἄλλος ἐγώ).

Besides, various sayings which in a way tell us about the ethical beliefs of the Pythagoreans had been written down in Pythagoras' model school. For example: "Don't poke the fire with a knife" meaning do not irritate an angry man. (Πῦρ μαχαίρᾳ μή σκαλεύειν). Also, "Don't eat your heart" (Καρδίαν μή ἐσθίειν) meaning do not trouble your heart with worries, etc.

In any case, "The Golden Epics" of Pythagoras, made up of 71 verses, are of admirable ethical content. These verses were most likely not written by Pythagoras, however, they faithfully embody his ethical teachings. The ethical teachings in the aforementioned work begin with the exhortation: "Honour the immortal gods and afterwards the glorious heroes ". Undoubtedly Pythagoras was religious and supported the ethics of heroism.

Politically, Pythagoras was as much an enemy of dictatorship as democracy. It was because of Polycrates' dictatorship that he left Samos and migrated to Croton in South Italy where he nevertheless did not manage to escape/get away from democracy. The democrats tore down and set fire to his school and at the same time murdered both Pythagoras himself and his pupils. In politics Pythagoras thought/preached the theory of the chosen/select which was talked about so much later and which was copied by the Italian philosopher Vilfredo Pareto, the sociologists of National Socialism/Nazism, Facicm and related ideologies.

Naturally, Pythagoras played an active part/role in the

state's public life. Indeed, by general acknowledgement of his authority, he managed to impose unity, to have the keeping of concubines recognized/considered as a punishable crime/a crime or an offence punishable by law, to have family bonds made stronger/strengthened, to have religious feeling made more intense/intensified and to have the individual and his position as a value of itself supplanted by the social whole (κοινωνική ὁλότης).

Pythagoras would hold up his school as an example to be imitated. His principles predominated in the strictest manner. In fact Pythagoras had established an original community of goods in his school; and this because he believed that the possession of even insignificant things causes disputes and disturbance/trouble. In the school "no one possessed a thing of his own ".

Pythagoras' political successes spread to other cities of Greater Greece. In Tarentum, Rhegion (present day Reggio), Himera, Metapontium,as well as elsewhere, the Pythagoreans preached/ disseminated/spread their social ideas and little by little came to dominate/prevail until they were unexpectedly destroyed by the democrats. The democrats never forgave Pythagoras for teaching: " τάς λεωφόρους μή βαδίζειν", that is, do not fall in with the opinion of the many and " τῶν δ' ἄλλων ἀρετῇ ποιοῦ φίλον ὅστις ἄριστος" (Golden Epics) meaning, make friends with those who excel in virtue, which ruled out the concept of the equality of man.

For the sake of history a few facts about the celebrated School of Pythagoras will be mentioned briefly. Before being accepted one had to undergo certain physical and intellectual tests. We do not know what exactly was tested/examined, however, we know that in the physical exercises wrestling was forbidden (because it was unworthy of men to roll about on the ground) and in the intellectual exercises one was asked about various subjects during a symposium. If he was accepted he was called auditor (ἀκουσματικός) and entered the first rank for which initiation lasted 2-5 years and during which time the pupils were forbidden to speak. They only listened to the moral teachings of Pythagoras as delivered by his assistants and did not have the right to discuss or object to what they heard. Besides, the principle/rule/law of "He said" (that is, Pythagoras said it and therefore it is so) was in effect. This very principle was introduced into sociological terminology through the term "the leader principle ". The pupils were supported by the common treasury where they had deposited their property.

After the necessary time had elapsed the pupils who where considered able were promoted and became members of the inner circle (ἐσωτερικοί). At this point they were allowed to hear Pythagoras himself and to teach pupils of the first rank as well as pupils of their own rank. Their basic concern was the elucidation of the lessons (geometry, music, astronomy, arithmetic, etc.). Finally there was a third rank, the members of which supervised and controlled the running of the school. Pythagoras had no secrets from them. In fact, they applied themselves to/dealt with/concerned themselves with the theories concerning the soul (psyche) which was believed to migrate from one body to another after the death of its bearer inasmuch as he led a sinful life. The soul sought to purify itself through its transmigrations. If the soul managed to purify itself then it would become one with the divinity after wandering about in the heaven for a while. Otherwise it would be condemned to the sufferings of

Tartarus. The successive transmigrations could last up to 3000 years. Pythagoras, then taught that the soul is immortal and that there is a reward for virtue and a punishment for sinful life. Christianity adheres to these religious beliefs, excepting the transmigration of souls. Christianity teaches that the Son of God incarnate, Christ suffered martyrdom to atone for man's Original Sin.

We must stress and pay special attention to the fact that Pythagoras used symbolism with either numbers or geometrical shapes for many reasons (security, simplicity, presentation, etc.). For example, justice was represented by the square. It would therefore show extreme naivete if we did not study the essential/true nature of his symbolism. It would be better to admit ignorance as to what Pythagoras' symbolism meant than to make up explanations/ interpretations.

A great deal is known about Pythagoras' private life. The most significant fact of all is that when he was in Egypt he associated with Egyptian priests and the Pharaoh Amasis. When Cambyses, king of Persia, overthrew the Pharaohs Pythagoras was taken captive and lived in Babylon for twelve years. He was finally freed through the intervention of the Greek Democedes who was the personal physician of the Persian king. Thereafter he lived in Samos until the age of 56 when, unwilling to tolerate Polycrates' dictatorship, he went to Delphi. After being harassed and dragged to court by the democrats he ended up in Greater Greece where he was assassinated. He is said to have attended lessons taught by Thales and Anaximander.

Philolaus (5th century B.C.)

According to some historians Philolaus came from Croton (Cf. Diogenes Laertius, VIII, 86) and according to others from Tarentum (Cf. Iamblichus, Vita Pythagorae). Nevertheless, the fact remains that, after the destruction of Pythagoras' school, he managed to escape to Thebes where he settled and established his own school. Evidently he taught successfully (among his pupils were Keves and Simmias who where both present at Socrates' last hours) and he applied himself to medicine beyond mathematics. Unfortunately of his two works, Bacchae and De Naturae which were written in the Doric dialect, only a few fragments remain. Undoubtedly the aforementioned works were very important; otherwise Plato would not have bought them at the high prices of 100 mna. We also know that Plato based his dialogue, Timaeus, on them.

As the Pythagoreans used to do so did Philolaus teach through riddles/stories, " δι' αἰνιγμάτων ἐδίδασκεν, καθάπερ ἦν ἔθος αὐτοῖς". He believed that the universe is unique: " ὁ κόσμος εἷς ἐστι " and that its development began in its middle, that is from a central point which is equidistant from the top and the bottom, " ἤρξατο δέ γίγνεσθαι ἀπό τοῦ μέσου καί ἀπό τοῦ μέσου εἰς τό ἄνω διά τῶν αὐτῶν τοῖς κάτω" (Bacchae). The fundamental unit/one from which the universe was produced was called Hestia: "Τό πρῶτο ἁρμοσθέν, τό ἕν, ἐν τῷ μέσῳ τῆς σφαίρας, Ἑστία καλεῖται". (Ibid). His opinion on the formation of the universe is also noteworthy. Philolaus believed that the universe is made up of a combination of the finite and infinity, " ἐξ ἀπείρων τε καί περαινόντων". (De Naturae). This is due to the fact that if everything was infinite then it would be impossible for us to perceive objects: " ἀρχήν γάρ οὐδέ τό γνωσούμενον ἐσσεῖται πάντων ἀπείρων ἐόντων". (Ibid).

Philolaus, of course, accepts the theory of numbers which are, essentially, the only inalterable/invariable/constant characteristics of matter. Besides, he gained reknown/became famous for his conviction that the earth moves and, in fact, moves in a circle: " περιφερομένην ". This information was handed down to us/given to us by Actius who received it from Theophrastus.

There were a few other famous Pythagoreans: Icetas, about whom Copernicus wrote in his De Revolutionibus Orbium Coelestium (1543): "He was the main-spring which started me thinking about movement of the earth"; Ecphantos, who spoke of the revolution of the earth; Archytas, who is considered the founder of the science of engineering; the architect Hippodamus, who presented an original concept about the ideal state; the sculptor Polyclitus from Argus, who in his work, Canon, discussed the proportions of the human figure; the tragic poet Ion from Chios; the illustrious physician Democedes; Alcmaeon, who founded physiology and performed the first surgical operation; Petron, who believed that many worlds existed in the universe; Hippasus and many others whose work is unknown but who are known to us only by name.

ELEATIC SCHOOL

Xenophanes (570-475 B.C.)

Xenophanes came from Colophon in Asia Minor. According to information provided by Theophrastus he had been a pupil of Anaximander's and had studied the ideas of the Ioniac philosophers. He left his native land when he was young, as soon as the Persians took possession of it. He began travelling until he finally settled in Elea in Greater Greece. It seems that while he was living at the court of the king of Syracuse Hieron who was a patron of the arts, he met Aeschylus, Pindar and Simonides. During his travels he covered his expenses by selling his poems, for Xenophanes had not only a great philosophical mind but a significant poetic talent as well.

Xenophanes' clarity of thought is evidenced by the bold certainty with which he fought against conventional concepts about the gods. Thus he turned against Homer and Hesiod whom he accused of assigning to the gods all those characteristics which bring disgrace and censure to men such as the fact that gods were involved in thievery, adultery and deceit . " Πάντα Θεοῖς ἀνέθηκαν Ὅμηρος,Ἡσίοδος τε, ὅσσα παρ' ἀνθρωπίσιν ὀνείδεα καί ψόγος ἐστιν, κλέπτειν, μοιχεύειν τε καί ἀλλήλοις ἀπατεύειν ". Xenophanes did not believe in many anthromorphous gods. God is one: " Εἷς Θεός μέγιστος" without any similarity to mortals in either body or spirit. " Οὔτε δέμας θνητοῖοιν ὁμοίοις οὐδέ νόημα". In fact, this god can see, hear and understand all things because he is all eye all ear all mind. This one god is all-powerful as well, " κράτιστος " and, through his spiritual powers, rules/governs/moves all things without effort: " ἀπάνευθε πόνοιο νόου φρενί πάντα κραδαίνει ". At the same time he manages to do all of the above without moving since, being all-present he is able to take care of everything/all things without going from place to place: " αἰεί δ' ἐν ταυτῷ μέμνει κινούμενος οὐδέν οὐδέ μετέρχεσθαι μέν ἐπιτρέπει ἄλλοτε ἄλλη ".

Xenophanes went on to say that God is the most perfect of beings and rules the world/universe as a result. He can only be one (alone) because it is inconceivable that there can exist many most perfect beings ruling at the same time. As to depicting God as having a specific form, Xenophanes observed/noted that we imagine God to be like us. To prove this point he cited the fact that the Ethiopians make their gods black whereas the Thraciens make them all fair. Besides, he maintained/claimed that if horses and oxen could depict their gods they would undoubtedly liken them to oxen and horses " ἵπποι μέν θ' ἵπποισι βόες δέ τε βουσίν ὁμοίας καί θεῶν ἰδέας ἔγραφον καί σώματ' ἐποίουν τοιαῦθ' οἷον περ καὐτοί δέμας εἶχον ἕκαστοι ".

According to one point of view, given to us by Aristotle in his Metaphysics and previously, by Plato in his Sophist, Xenophanes identifies God with the world and beings in a pantheistic maker. In other words/That is to say he accepts that the being is one and that is everything in accordance with his theory "ἕν εἶναι τό πᾶν" meaning that everything is one substance. Indeed this one which, as we have said, is everything, is God: " τό ἕν τοῦτο καί πᾶν τόν Θεόν". (Theophrastus). Nevertheless, as evidenced by a fragment, Xenophanes accepted the concept that everything comes from the earth and returns to the earth: " ἐκ γαίης γάρ πάντα καί εἰς τήν γῆν πάντα τελευτᾶ " a view which Christianity presented in the phrase: " χοῦς ἐσμέν καί εἰς χοῦν ἀπελευσόμεθα ".

Xenophanes also overthrew the popular belief that all

the comforts of civilization were given to man by the gods. According to him the progress/evolution of civilization is not a result of the philanthropy/kindness of the gods but rather (the result) of man's continual quest. As time goes by man discovers/invents improvements thus raising the standard/level of his civilization: " Οὔτοι ἀπ'ἀρχῆς πάντα θεά θνητοῖς ὑπέδειξαν, ἀλλά χρόνῳ ζητοῦντες ἐφευρίσκουν ἄμεινον ". The aforementioned interpretation of the genesis/origin and development of civilization (which holds true even today) thus gives Xenophanes the title of "first philosopher of civilization" by right.

Xenophanes was also an admirable poet who wrote epics, elegies and "σιλλούς" (biting/teaching hexameter verse). He praised the sweet flower-scented wine which promised not to betray the thick honey and the light-coloured bread. Elsewhere he attributed the destruction of Colophon to the fact that its inhabitants had stopped being inured to hardships and had succumbed to indolence. In another poem he praised wisdom which he placed above/valued more than physical strength/vigour.

Parmenides (540-470 B.C.).

Parmenides was born in Elea, a city in Greater Greece founded by colonists from Phocaea. It seems that, being born of an aristocratic family, he involved himself in politics/concerned himself with politics; but the Pythagorean Aminias* urged him to abandon the troubles of politics and devote himself to the quiet life of a philosopher. So, Parimenides studied Xenophanes' teachings based upon which he presented the Eleatic philosophy, as the static view of the universe is called.

Even though Parmenides abandoned politics, he made laws for his country and through his serious character had great influence on public matters in which he always participated against democratic tendencies. He was so impressive a personage that Plato, in his Θεαίτητον wrote that he inspired Socrates' respect.

As was the custom in his time, Parmenides presented his ideas in a poem which can be divided into two parts. In the first he dealt with/included all that is real and in the second he described glory, that is, the different erroneous ideas that mortals/people have (on the subject).

The basic concept of Parmenides' teachings is the being. When he speaks of a being he exclusively means that which is complete or full, meaning matter which takes up space.

The non-being, meaning empty space, did not exist for Parmenides. Furthermore, by extension of his basic concept of the being, he believed that the being has/had neither end nor beginning for the simple reason that it could not/cannot come from a non-being nor can/could it end up as a non-being. Therefore the being is/was "unborn"-

"ἀγέννητος", "indestructible" - "ἀνώλεθρον" complete in members (inseparable completeness) and "untroubled" - " ἀτρεμές " (undisturbed). Moreover, it is/was a constant presence which never was, and we therefore cannot be spoken of in terms of the past, and never will be, thus never having a future. It exists as a continuous present with a past or a future: " τό ὄν οὐδέ ποτ' ἦν οὐδ' ἔσται, ἐπεί νῦν ἐστιν ὁμοῦ πᾶν, ἕν, συνεχές". Besides, the being is eternally the very same, immovable, inalterable and indivisible because nothing is capable of changing it, of moving it or of dividing it. As to Parmenides' epistemology we have this basic fact to present: He believed that whatever is subject to/falls under/is perceived by our comprehension/intellect exists. Intellect is identified with existence. Or in other words, that which does not exist cannot be comprehended/understood. We reach the concept of the being through the word (διά τοῦ λόγου) which means the being. On the other hand our senses, which make birth, decay, and change perceptible to us, are sources of deception. We therefore realize that Parmenides distrusted the senses because the present changes whereas there exists/is an unchangeable/unchanging being. Heraclitus similarly distrusted the senses but for exactly the opposite reason: the senses, he said, present a stillness while in reality there is eternal motion.

In any case, Parmenides recognizes one sole reality: the reality which we are led to by the word and which is the undisturbed, nonchangeable and indivisible being. On the contrary, our senses present the fallacious /fraudulist /deceptive world of appearances which, however, bears a certain resemblance to reality but is not true reality. A person who is not versed in philosophy sees this false reality in which there exist birth and decay whereas the philosopher, through the word, sees that true reality, which truly exists, wherein absolute stability prevails.

Zeno of Elea (464 or 490-? B.C.)

Zeno, like Parmenides, was born in Elea. We know very little about his life. Nevertheless, we are informed that he was Teleutagoros' son, Parmenides' pupil and Pericles' teacher. Hermippus, as well as Souidas, mention that Zeno fought against Nearchus' dictatorship. In the end, he was caught/captured/ seized/arrested and while he was being interrogated he cut off his tongue (so not to betray his companions) and spat it out in the face of the dictator who ordered his execution by squeezing/compression in a huge mortar.

Plato and Aristotle presented a few of Zeno's teachings. In fact, Aristotle considers Zeno the inventor of dialectic. In his Physics and elsewhere Stagiritis opposed Zeno's contentions/assertions/ allegations as regards space, time, and motion and thus we indirectly can infer what the Eleatic's teachings were. We can do likewise with Platos' writings. We can gather some information from his dialogue entitled Parmenides and thus learn that many people, among them Socrates, attended when Zeno taught in Athens. Unfortunately, except for certain fragments found in other writers, Zeno's writings were lost.

In any case, Zeno presented a series of considerable arguments through which he proved that motion and change do not exist in the world/Cosmos. Note that even though science accepts Aristotle's corrections it still has not offered/given a satisfactory reply to Zeno's arguments which are the following:

If we take a dimension we can divide it ad infinitum. If we continue this infinite division we reach/end up with nothing which is, most certainly, the last point in division/the utmost division. Therefore, a dimension is the sum of infinite nothings and so dimension does not exist. Since dimension does not exist motion does not either because motion without a dimension to go through/travel in/cover cannot be perceived.

Zeno applied a similar train of thought when he said that one must first travel/cover half the distance in order to cover the distance A to B. However, before covering that half, one must cover half of that half. Before covering half of the half of the whole, one must cover half of the half of the half and so on ad infinitum. How, then, can one cover the distance from A to B if one must move ad infinitum, covering infinite halves of halves?

Zeno's roof known as the "proof/argument of the arrow" is also important. Zeno maintained that an arrow that has been shot does not move because time is divided into infinitesimal small moments/ instants/units of time which cannot be further divided after a certain point. So, at a certain point in time the arrow is in one position, in one locus (τοπικόν σημεῖον) and if it is in one position it is not moving. If the arrow is moving then it is not in one place/position, which is impossible. To refute this argument Aristotle himself asserted that Zeno was mistaken since time, like every other dimension, is infinitely divisible. This view which is considered to be correct even today, leads us to a dead-end because we inevitably come back to Zeno's argument according to which when we divide a dimension infinitely we reach/end up with nothing and, as a result, we conclude that dimension is the total of infinite nothings therefore dimension does not exist. To prove the contradiction between motion and reality Zeno asked: if equal distances are to be covered in equal amounts of time at an equal speed, then why does a body pass in front of another twice as fast as when it was motionless, if it is going in the opposite direction?

Besides this argument, the argument called "Achilles and the tortoise" is also famous. According to this argument the fleet-footed Achilles will never be able to reach the tortoise (even though he is running twelve times as fast) if the tortoise precedes him in space because when he reaches the tortoise's position, the tortoise will be in another position.

Although an admirer of Zenos, Aristotle obstinately fought against his theories concerning the non-existence of motion, developing his theories as to dynamic and real infinity. In spite of this, those of Zeno's theories which so far have not been scientifically disproved have benefited science enormously. Zeno was the first to present the theory of relativity, a fact accepted by Dills/Deels/Deals/Diels. The theory of relativity appeared especially with the argument of the coincidence of (the) half and (the) double distance/space/interval. And, generally, the theory appeared throughout his works wherein he maintained that all human knowledge is hypothetical, meaning that it is based on a supposition and therefore both it (knowledge) and its conclusions are of a relative nature.

Melissus (430-? B.C.)

Another famous Eleatic is Melissus of Samos. In his work "De Naturae ἤ περί τοῦ ὄντος" he supported the belief that whatever existed, existed and will exist perpetually /eternally. Inasmuch as each thing was created through birth/genesis, it would logically follow that it did not exist before its birth. On the other hand, if it did not exist it would not be possible for it to have been created out of nothing: "ἀεί ἦν καί ἀεί ἔσται. Εἰ γάρ ἐγένετο ἀναγκαῖον ἐστι πρίν γενέσθαι εἶναι μηδέν εἰ τοίνον μηδέν ἦν, οὐδαμά ἄν γένοιτο οὐδέν ἐκ μηδενός ". The reason that Being will exist forever, that is, will never end, must be attributed to the conviction that it is impossible for a non-existent thing to be/become/be born. Nevertheless Melissus saw the infinity as well as the eternity of Being. He said that a thing cannot be eternal if it is not present at all points: "Οὐ γάρ ἀεί εἶναι ἀνυστόν, ὅτι μή πᾶν ἐστι ".Therefore the Being is eternal as regards time, infinite as regards space, one and integral the same as itself: " οὕτως οὖν ἀΐδιόν ἐστι καί ἄπειρον καί ὅμοιον πᾶν ".

As to epistemology, Melissus denies the trustworthiness of the senses which present us with a reality which does not truly exist. The inability of the senses to present the true nature of beings is proved by the fact that beings change. That is, the same beings, ourselves, as, for example, the senses of sight, present things differently every so often/now and then. That which our sight perceives to be white, it may later perceive to be another colour. We may therefore infer that the original assertion which the sense of sight made as to the nature of being did not correspond to the truth since, if everything our sight told us were true, no changes would be observed: " δῆλον τοῖνον ὅτι οὐκ ὀρθῶς ἑωρῶμεν... οὐ γάρ ἄν μετέπιπτεν εἰ ἀληθῆ ἦν ". Therefore, for Melissus, the validity of the senses as evidence of truth, is definitely dismissed/rejected. As to his political beliefs Melissus was a great believer in patriotism. As a matter of fact he, himself, was of great service to Samos when, acting as admiral, he defeated the Athenian fleet. In the end, however, he was defeated by Pericles.

HERACLITEAN SCHOOL

Heraclitus (544-484 B.C.)

Although born in Ephesus Heraclitus was of Athenian descent. His family was descended from King Codros whose son, Androclus, built Ephesus. In contrast to the preceding philosophers, Heraclitus spoke authoritatively and sententiously. Besides being original in his style (which Nietzsche faithfully imitated), he showed originality in his presentation of meaning. His meaning was hidden in the depths of the powerful words which he used and which he often placed (in such order/so) as to make comprehension most difficult. It was because of this that he got/acquired the title of "obscure". Livy was the fist to give him that title for he did not manage to understand him.

The great concentration of meaning, the use of etymological forms, and the unity of the meaning of Heraclitus' aphorisms make it so difficult to understand his writings that even Socrates himself, on returning Heracletus' De Naturae to Euripides, said: "῞Α μέν συνῆκα γενναῖα οἶμαι δέ καί ἅ μή συνῆκα" (Diogenes Laertius) meaning, ("I found) whatever I understand daring and I think that what I did not understand must be daring, too ".

In any case, that which we definitely know is that Heraclitus taught that war is the creator of world order. The struggle must never end because if it does then the evolution and advancement of values which are ensured only by continuous struggle, will stop. War is the father of all things and king of all beings. It renders some gods and other mortals/men; it makes some slaves and others freemen: " Πόλεμος πάντων μέν πατήρ ἐστι, πάντων δέ βασιλεύς, και τούς μέν θεούς ἔδειξε τούς μέν ἀνθρώπους, τούς μέν δούλους ἐποίησε τούς δέ ἐλευθέρους" (53).

Heraclitus' approval of war, that is life's constant struggle through which progress is realized by the prevalence of that which is superior, is evident by the vehemence with which he attacked Homer and Archilochus both of whom had spoken against war. Heraclitus sought to have them excluded/expelled from poetry competitions and have them slapped. " Τόν δε Ὅμηρον ἄξιον ἐκ τῶν ἀγώνων ἐκβάλλεσθαι καί ραπίζεσθαι καί Ἀρχίλοχον ὁμοίως ".(42) Moreover, he established the notion of the fighter/the fighting man as a measure of merit, proclaiming/declaring that both gods and men honour those who fall in battle: " Ἀρηιφάτους θεοί τιμῶσι καί ἄνθρωποι". (24) These theories concerning a general struggle as a factor which helps the hierarchy and order of Nature materialize were copied by Darwin in his theory concerning the struggle for existence, and by Spencer in his theory concerning the survival of the fittest.

Heraclitus believed in God whom he considered as a reality independent of and against to beings, and therefore insurpassable. At the same time he maintains that God is the one and only Wise One that knows how to rule everything down to the last detail: " Ἕν τό σοφόν, ἐπίσταται γνώμην ἐτεῇ κυβερνῆσαι πάντα, διά πάντων ".(41) God's wisdom cannot be compared with man's, as none of His qualities can be compared with man's. If we dare (to) compare them then even the wisest man will prove himself nothing more than an ape in all respects before God: "᾽Ανθρώπων ὁ σοφώτατος πρός Θεόν πίθηκος φανεῖται καί σοφία καί κάλλει καί τοῖς ἄλλοις πᾶσιν ".(83)

Evidently Heraclitus acknowledged the existence of divine providence which, as he wrote, tends all the animals on earth which are led to their food by God who guides them as a shepherd guides his flock: "Πᾶν ἑρπετόν (ἑρπετόν means an animal that moves on the earth) Θεοῦ πληγῇ νέμεται" (11). We could parallel this fragment of Heraclitus with Matthew 6, verse 26, where Christ says that God takes care of/looks after the food of the roosters of heaven: " Πατήρ σας ὁ οὐράνιος τρέφει αὐτά".

Heraclitus founded two other important principles as well as the principle of war/struggle. The first of these is the principle of the unity of contrasts. According to this principle things can/may exhibit contrasting views and yet make up a unity in the end. The final unity of contrasts is God who embraces the total of all contrasts. He is day-night, summer-winter, war-peace, hunger-satiation: " Ὁ Θεός ἡμέρα εὐφρόνη, χειμών,θέρος, πόλεμος, εἰρήνη, κόρος, λιμός".(67) The second of these principles is the principle of the constant evolution of things. The famous phrase "All is flux" is attributed to Heraclitus through a phase found in Aristotle's Metaphysics (6) wherein it is mentioned that ever since his youth Plato believed the opinion of Heraclitus' supporters that everything is constantly flowing. Indeed Heraclitus taught/preached the constant flow of things but at the same time he accepted that stability as existing in the body and manifesting itself through the word/speech which implies the essence of reality which forever remains constant.

Heraclitus taught that the world originated from fire and will end in fire. It is born of fire, and burning itself out, it is destroyed so as to be created again from fire, and so on. These unending changes, however, occur in a fixed manner. In any case, the world was not created by either God or man but existed and will exist forever: " Κόσμον τόν δε, τόν αὐτόν ἁπάντων, οὔτε τις θεῶν οὔτε ἀνθρώπων ἐποίησεν, ἀλλ' ἦν ἀεί καί ἔστιν καί ἔσται πῦρ άείζωον, άπτόμενον μέτρα καί ἀποσβεννύμενον μέτρα".(30)

Heraclitus believed that a process made up of "χρησμοσύνη" (fire takes on the shape/form of an element) and of "satiation"-"κόρον" (the elements return to fire) operates in the universe. This process has been proven to hold true as to primordeal matter which is thin/rare and moves vigorously. When through its motion this primordeal matter accumulates (in one place)/condenses forms of matter which are inversely proportionate to the accumulation which has taken place are created. When, on the contrary, rarefication takes place, then the forms return to their original condition which is common to all and which, according to Heraclitus, is called "fire". Heraclitus called the primordial matter of beings "fire" because of all known elements it is the most mobile and least stable. Therefore inexpert interpreters of Heraclitus give his use of the word "pyr" the ordinary meaning of "fire".

But let us now come to Heraclitus' political beliefs which fortunately are absolutely clear:

He hated democracy which does away with personalities through a false equality. Heraclitus believed and proclaimed/declared that the many are evil whereas there are few good people: "οἱ πολλοί κακοί, ὀλίγοι δέ ἀγαθοί" (104). He also denied the supremacy of the majority who are not like the very best of men who seek eternal glory rather than transient/perishable things. The many, said Heraclitus, are satisfied with being satiated just like beasts: " Aἱροῦνται γάρ ἕν ἀντί ἁπάντων οἱ ἄριστοι, κλέος ἀέναον θνητῶν, οἱ δέ πολλοί κεκόρηνται ὅκωσπερ κτήνεα " (29). Authority/power of government should therefore not be given to them but to the few or even to the one who will be worth then thousand if he is of the very best of men: " Εἷς ἐμοί μύριοι, ἐάν ἄριστος ᾖ" (49). The will of this best of men is law which we ought to obey:"Νόμος καί βουλή πείθεσθαι ἑνός" (33).

Heraclitus' hatred of democracy is repressively released/let loose in the case of Hermodorus' exile. Heraclitus said "The Ephessians deserve to have all their adults hanged and to leave the government/administration of their city in the hands of the minors because they exiled Hermodorus who was the most useful citizen by saying, There should not be a most useful person among us and if there is one he should leave, to go live in another country with other people" .

"Ἄξιον Ἐφεσσίοις ἡβηδόν ἀπάγξασθαι πᾶσι καί τοῖς ἀνήβοις πόλιν καταλιπεῖν, οἵτινες Ἑρμόδωρον ἄνδρα ἑαυτῷ ὀνήιστον ἐξέβαλον φάντες ἡμέων μηδέ εἷς ἀνήηστος ἔστω, εἰ δέ μή ἄλλη τε και μετ' ἄλλων ".(121)For history's sake we mention the fact Hermodorus was a legislator/ lawgiver and, according to Pliny, he wrote/drew up/ composed the Roman Twelve Tables.

Heraclitus hated dictatorship as well. He placed himself unreservedly in favour of/for the rule/government by a minority of the elite (ὀλίγων καί ἀγαθῶν). The German philosopher Zeller mentioned Heraclitus' political views. In his book Die Philosophie der Griechen in lhrer Geschichtlichen Entwicklung he says that Heraclitus, "being born an aristocrat, was as much an enemy of dictatorship, which was imposed on his country for some time, as of democracy whose deeds disgusted him so much that he withdrew to the isolation of the temple of Artemis ".

CONNECTIVE SCHOOL

Empedocles (495-435 B.C.)

Empedocles came from Acragas and took an active part in its political life. Some people who confuse his love of the people with democracy maintain that he had democratic convictions; however, he did not believe in democracy. As a political man he fought against the dictatorial system of government which had been imposed by the "oligarchy of the thousand" and managed to overthrow it. " Ὁ Ἐμπεδοκλῆς καί τό τῶν χιλίων ἄθροισμα κατέλυσε συνεστώς ἐπί τρία ἔτη". (Diogenes Laertius, VIII, 66). When the inhabitants of Acragas offered him the kingship Empedocles refused because he had a different mission to perform. Together with many faithful followers he went from city to city where he taught, philosophized, cured the sick, studied the problems, and so on. He himself did not believe in democratic equality. Feeling himself intellectually superior to the others, he went so far as to ask his fellow-citizens to consider him a god. "Καί δόξαν περί αὐτοῦ κατασχεῖν ὡς περί θεοῦ βουλόμενος" Suidas. He explicitly made his view known in Fragment 112 of his work <u>Purifications</u> (Καθαρμοί) where he says that he is a god and not a mortal. " Ἐγώ δ' ὑμῖν θεός ἄμβροτος οὐκέστι". Finally his fellow-citizens most democratically not only exiled him but also refused to allow him to return to Acragas in spite of his touching efforts to do so. So he died, in exile, in the Peloponesse. " Ὕστερον μέντοι ἀντέστησαν αὐτοῦ τῇ καθόδῳ οἱ τῶν ἐχθρῶν ἀπόγονοι. Διόπερ εἰς Πελοπόννησον ἀποχωρήσας ἐτελεύτησεν" (Diogenes Laertius VIII, 67).

Empedocles held that the Universe is composed of four elements: air, fire, earth and water. It is from these elements, which Empedocles called "roots", that the various beings are created by means of two forces called Love and Strife ("Φιλότης-Νεῖκος"). Love brings them (the elements) together whereas Strife separates them. The one is love and the other hate; therefore the genesis and decay of beings are nothing more than the union and separation of the "roots" which are unchangeable elements.

More specifically, Empedocles taught that living beings originally were masses without a specific appearance/shape but evolved into certain/definite forms as time went by. Moreover, Empedocles' teaching as regards knowledge is very important too. He taught that we perceive an element/know something through the same element/thing which exists in us. This is the theory which has recently reappeared the theory of intuition (enaesthesis-θεωρία ἐναισθήσεως) , according to which the subject recognizes the object by means of the same qualities which exist in both. In fact, Empedocles descriptively formulated the theory of intuition by saying that we recognize/perceive/come to know the earth, water, affection etc. through the earth, water, affection etc. which exist in us. ("Γαίῃ μέν γάρ γαίαν ὀπώπαμεν, ὕδατι δ'ὕδωρ, στοργήν δέ στοργῇ").

Nevertheless, Empedocles was not a monist. He believed in dualism as evidenced by the fact that he accepted the existence of the material world parallel to the existence of the blessed spirits, the daemones, as he called souls. These daemones are immortal and live most happily in their own community. However, if they sin while in their own community then they "fall" from the superior kingdom of the daemones and enter the material world where they assume the form of plants, animals or humans and are forced to wander in the Valley of Adversity (Ἄτης λειμῶνα) until they are purified. Finally, we could say that Empedocles was, in a way, the one who reconciled the theories of Heraclitus and Parmenides: the one supporting eternal motion and the other eternal immobility.

Scientific thought and mysticism were magnificently combined in the person of Empedocles. His declaration to his pupil Pausanias typefies the supernatural aspect of his personality. Empedocles promised Pausanias that through his teachings he would learn of medicines against illness and old age, he would be able to master the winds and he would even be able to bring souls back to earth from Hades [resurrect the dead]. "Φάρμακα δ' ὅσσα γεγᾶσι κακῶν καί γήρατος, ἄλκαρ πεύσῃ...Παύσῃς δ' ἀκαμάτων ἀνέμων μένος...ἄξεις δ' ἐξ ἀΐδιο καταφθινομένου μένος ἄνδρος..." (111).

Moreover, Empedocles believed in the transmigration of souls which he presented most poetically in the following verses: "Ἤδη γάρ ποτ' ἐγώ γενόμην κοῦρος τε καί κόρη τε θάμνος τ' οἰωνός τε καί ἔναλος ἔλλοπος ἰχθύς" (117). Which, translated means, I have already existed as a youth and maiden, as a bush and as a bird and as a silent fish swimming in the sea. It is through these repeated transmigrations that man is purified and becomes, in turn, a prophet, a minstrel, a physician, a ruler, and, in the end attains divinity.

Empedocles' death was legendary. Diogenes Laertius recorded it as occurring as follows. After resurrecting a lifeless woman called Panthia he remained near the attar where he sacrificed to the gods. At midnight a loud voice calling Empedocles was heard. At the same time, as recounted by a servant who was an eyewitness, celestial light and the glow of torches poured out from the sky. Empedocles disappeared and was never seen again. "Τῶν οἰκετῶν τις ἔφη μέσων νυκτῶν φωνή ὑπερμεγέθους ἀκοῦσαι προκαλουμένης

Ἐμπεδοκλέα, εἶτα ἐξαναστάς ἑωρακέναι φῶς οὐράνιον καί λαμπάδων φέγγος, ἄλλο δέ μηδέν ".

Anaxagoras (500-428 B.C.)

Anaxagoras was born in Clazomenae in Asia Minor. He was descended from an aristocratic family but he was never directly involved in politics. When he left his home town and went to Athens he became good friends with Pericles to whom he taught rhetoric as Plato says in his Phaedrus. He was also a friend of Euripides' who transferred Anaxagoras' views to his poetic works.

Anaxagoras believed that genesis and decay do not exist. That which truly exists is a mixing and separation of the minute particles of matter which are infinite in numbers and varied in quality. The union of particles is what we call genesis and their division/separation is what we call decay. This is what really happens and so we mistakenly use the verbs to become/be created/born and to be lost because nothing is in fact created or lost. Everything makes its appearance after the admixture or withdrawal of elements which already exist. Therefore it would be correct indeed if we were to use the word admixture in place of genesis and if we were to speak of separation rather than decay. " Τό δέ γένεσθαι καί ἀπόλλυσθαι οὐκ ὀρθῶς νομίζουσιν οἱ Ἕλληνες οὐδέν γάρ χρῆμα γίνεται οὐδέ ἀπόλλυται ἀλλ' ἀπ' ἐόντων χρημάτων συμμίγεταί τε καί διακρίνεται. Καί οὕτως ἄν ὀρθῶς καλοῖεν τό τε γίνεσθαι συμμίγεσθαι καί τό ἀπόλλυσθαι διακρίνεσθαι " (C 17).So, Anaxagoras believed that matter, pre-existing as an undefined mixture of minor particles which are infinite in quantity and of all kinds in quality, makes the various forms of existence appear through the admixture or separation of the aforementioned particles which Anaxagoras called "chremata".

The undefined mixture of matter fills the universe

without leaving any empty space. A superior force causes the admixture and separation of the particles. This superior force is infinite, free of all other elements, self-existent, and the sovereign of all things, determining all happenings. This superior force which is an independent substance, different from matter and conscious of itself, was called "nous" (mind) by Anaxagoras. The mind is the principle through which order and harmony in the world are secured. Besides, the mind is that which guarantees purposeful actions, that is, deeds, in accordance with intentions. That is to say, nothing happens by chance. Each occurrence tends to fulfil a purpose either consciously as human deeds do, or unconsciously, as does plants' absorption of nutrients which contribute to their growth. So, the world has two components: mind and matter. The mind set the mixture of matter into motion and since then, the world and the various beings have been created by the admixture and separation of the minute particles.

We should stress the fact that since the mind is a completely immaterial being according to Anaxagoras it may be inferred that the νοῦς- "nous" (mind) is what later came to be known as spirit thus rightfully granting him/Anaxagoras the title of the founder of spiritualism. The mind gives rise to a force whose aim is to fulfil predetermined goals. As a result Anaxagoras can also claim the title of the founder of the technological view of the universe/world according to which the motions or actions of beings and the entire universe/world do not occur by chance but rather to certain ends (end=τέλος).

As a philosopher Anaxagoras was attracted/touched by the theoretical life to which purely theoretical research leads. Perhaps that is why he ignored politics as well as the management of his huge estate. Nevertheless he held aristocratic views and it was due to this that he was tried and imprisoned ostensibly for impiety. Evidently, with Pericles' help, he escaped and went to Lampsacus where he remained until his death and where he was greatly honoured by the inhabitants.

Anaxagoras' basic/fundamental view that the particles of matter make up an undefined mixture wherein we cannot distinguish qualities because of the imperfection of our senses arose from the following observation. He observed that when man receives food of a definite quality, e.g. bread, this food creates different qualities, e.g. nails, flesh, bones, nerves, etc. "Καί τροφῆς τῆς αὐτῆς, προσφερομένης οἷον ἄρτου, πολλά καί ὀνόμοια γίνεται, σάρκες, ὀστᾶ, φλέβες, νεῦρα, τρίχες, ὄνυχες ". (Simplicius). So, these various qualities are contained in or rather are inherent to bread without our being able to distinguish. It is by means of the function or rather the process of nutrition that particles of each quality are gathered together in different parts of the body and so we are in a position to see flesh, bones, nails, etc. Generally, everything which appears/is perceived (even colours and smells) is inherent to the mixture of particles which then gives it off/emits it under certain circumstances. The minute particles (chremata) are different from Leucippus' atoms in that Anaxagoras considered chremata to be of various kinds whereas Leucippus considered atoms to be the same.

Anaxagoras also presented admirable views as to the epistemological problem. As Theophrastus mentions in his On the Senses (Περί αἰσθήσεων). Anaxagoras believed that like is immoved by like " τό ὅμοιον ἀπαθές ὑπό τοῦ ὁμοίου ". That is to say that a substance has no effect on its like. For example, if we drink water which is at body temperature then we shall not become aware of either heat or cold. Therefore perception/sensation is the result of the effect/influence of things which are unlike. Nevertheless our senses are imperfect and so they cannot show us the reality which truly exists. In order to prove the deficiency of our senses Anaxagoras performed the following experiment. He took two containers, the one with/containing a white liquid and the other a black liquid. He then added a small quantity of the other to each and noted that the colours did not change; however, at the same time it was impossible for him to distinguish the small quantity he had poured into each container. This inability was due to the imperfection of the sense of sight. " Eἰ γάρ δύο λάβοιμεν χρώματα, μέλαν καί λευκόν καί εἶτα ἐκ θατέρου εἰς θάτερον κατά σταγόνα παρεγχέοιμεν, οὐ δυνήσεται ἡ ὄψις διακρίνει τάς παρά μικρόν μεταβολάς, καίπερ πρός την φύσιν ὑποκειμένας". (Sextus Empiricus προς μαθ. VII, 90). Since the inability of the senses to lead us to sure knowledge was stressed and proven, it was concluded that the mind is the means by which the truth is checked because it is absolutely free from/of the admixture of particles of matter whereas the sensory organs contain various particles which interfere with perfect perception. However, the senses are not epistemologically annihilated because they, too, help in the search for truth by presenting us with the phenomena which we start with in order to find the substantial reality of beings.

ATOMIC SCHOOL

Leucippus (5th cent. B.C.)

Unfortunately very little is known about Leucippus who was Democritus' teacher. Nevertheless from the information we have it seems that he was approximately a contemporary of Anaxagoras' and Thales' fellow countryman. Epicurus even went so far as to think that he never existed. However, he was wrong because many eye-witness accounts as well as historical research have proven that he was a real person. It is considered likely that Epicurus was misled by the fact that at that time the writings of Leucippus were found in the same book as those of Democritus.

Leucippus founded a philosophical school at Abdera and published its views in two important works. Unfortunately nothing but a few words have been saved of the one called The Great Cosmos-Μέγας Διάκοσμος. His second work has also been lost except from one phrase which expresses the entire content of the principle of causility which was later reproduced by non-Greek (ξένοι) philosophers. The phrase states that nothing happens without a cause, but everything happens because of a definite cause and by necessity. "Οὐδέν χρῆμα μάτην γίγνεται ἀλλά πάντα ἐκ λόγου τε καί ὑπ' ἀνάγκης ".

Finding himself in Elea following Zeno's teaching, Leucippus disagreed with him as to his idea that bodies are infinitely divisible. Leucippus maintained that we reach a minimum through constant bisection. It is impossible to further bisect this minimum because there is no empty space in it to make the division/incision (τομή) feasible. Leucippus called this minimum "atom". The sum of these atoms makes up what Parmenides called being. Atoms are neither created nor destroyed. They can be distinguished from each other not by/through qualitative difference but by/through their position, order-"τάξις" and shape. The universe and the objects contained in it are nothing more than compositions of atoms. So, atoms must move but in order to have motion we must necessary have empty space. Leucippus absolutely agreed with these findings and added that motion is eternal/perpetual, that is, without beginning or end. The elements, therefore, which make up the atomic theory are atoms, empty space and perpetual motion. Leucippus and his pupil Democritus undoubtedly founded the atomic theory solely on whose views the new atomic theory and research were based, as Gobertz acknowledges in his book, The Greek Thinkers - Οἱ Ἕλληνες στοχασταί.

Democritus (460-370 B.C.)

Democritus came from Abdera which was located between Macedonia and Thrace. He set out on long journeys early in his youth. He visited Egypt and Persia and, it is said, he even reached India. It seems that he competed against the local geometers while in Egypt and utterly defeated them, a deed which he was proud of. " Καί γραμμέων συνθέσιος μετ' ἀποδείξεως οὐδείς κώ με παρήλλαξεν οὐδ' οἱ Αἰγυπτίων καλεόμενοι 'Αρπε-δονάπται ". (Clement of Alexandria, Str. I, 13). Meaning, no man showed himself superior to me in the competition of geometrical designs based on proof, not even those in Egypt who are called Arpedonaptae (earth measurers).

When Democriuts returned to his home town he had already squandered his fortune and so his brother supported him. However, since the law provided that anyone who squandered the family fortune not be buried, Democritus read a work of his "The Great Cosmos" to the inhabitants of Abder in order to avoid this shame. The inhabitants were so impressed that they gave him 100 talents as a prize. He also visited Athens where no one paid attention to him. This was to result in/give rise to his complaint: I came to Athens and no one recognized me. "Ἦλθον γάρ εἰς 'Αθήνας καί οὐ τίς μέ ἔγνωκεν".(Diogenes Laertius, IX, 30).

Democritus is well known for his theories on atoms. He gained world-wide fame and his name is inseparably bound to the atom. In the fist place, he believed that genesis and decay do not exist. He accepted the existence of the empty space/void and the full/occupied space. Up to here we can see a similarity to the theories of Parmenides, with the difference that Democritus gave his empty space (Parmenides' non being) existence. According to Democritus the non-being exists just as the being exists. Non-being is empty space, the void. Occupied space, Democritus maintained, is made up of countless particles which are separated by the void and which are indivisible because they occupy/take up all their space so that there is no empty space in them to make their division possible. These particles, which Democritus called "atoms", are unborn, imperishable, uniform (distinguishable only by size and shape), at the same time not susceptible to qualitative changes save for displacement, and, all this, precisely because they are indivisible. Therefore, the development of beings is nothing more than the joining of separated atoms and their decay the separation of unified atoms. The properties of beings depend on how the atoms are placed and the size of the atoms. The atoms are in constant motion in the void thanks to their different weights which are due to these differences in size since they are of the same kind.

Democritus' moral beliefs are likewise noteworthy. He believed in the good of friendship to such a degree that he declared that life is not worth living in one does not have even one good friend. "Ζῆν οὐκ ἄξιος ὅπως μηδέ εἷς ἐστι χρηστός φίλος" (9).One ought to have a wise friend, it is better to have one such friend than to have many foolish ones. " Ἑνός φιλίη ξυνετοῦ κρέσσων ἀξυνέτων ἁπάντων" (98). Democritus considered the following to be important in a friendship: similar ideas, and similar opinion make a friendship, " ὁμοφροσύνη φιλίην ποιεῖ" (186).Moreover, he proclaimed the sovereignity of the fighting spirit. The ideal of struggle ranked before the comfortable life, which he despised; on the other hand he esteemed the heroic life. He renounced eudaemonism saying that it is not only he who wins in war who is brave but also he who wins the battle against pleasure. In fact, he expressively said that some men happen to be leader but are women's slaves, taking women to be the symbol of pleasure. "'Ανδρεῖος οὐχ ὁ τῶν πολεμίων, ἀλλά καί ὁ τῶν ἡδονῶν κρέσσων. Ἔνιοι δέ πολίων μέν δεσπόζουσι, γυναιξί δέ δουλεύουσιν " (124).

Politically, Democritus supported the rule of the mighty for, as he says point blank, authority naturally belongs to the most powerful/one who is most/more powerful: " φύσει τό ἄρχειν οἰκήιον τῷ κρέσσονι" (261) Furthermore he (justly) supported the view that it is bad/evil to be governed by one's inferiors. " Χαλεπόν ἄρχεσθαι ὑπό χείρονος " (49). As a result Democritus political beliefs can only be considered anti-democratic since elsewhere he calls for obedience not to the majority but to the leader and the wisest man (47). In addition to this he did not accept the concept of democratic equality among men. He taught that whoever follows the opinions of the many is naive and on the other hand, whoever believes only those who have been tested (those whom Socrates later called connoisseurs) is prudent. " Μή πᾶσιν, ἀλλά τοῖς δοκίμοισι πιστεύειν τό μέν γάρ εὔηθες τό δέ σωφρονέοντος " (66). Besides, in many of his sayings, Democritus indignantly turned against those who are foolish asking that they not have any authority because, upon close examination, it will be found that it is to their benefit not to govern but rather to be governed. "Κρέσσον ἄρχεσθαι τοῖς ἀνοήτοισιν ἤ ἄρχειν " (75). Democritus' fear that foolish and bad people will take office is spread through his political counsel. When bad people are given authority the more unworthy they are the more they are governed by indifference and are filled with foolishness and impudence once in power. "Οἱ κακοί ἰόντες εἰς τάς τιμάς ὀνόσῳ ἄν μᾶλλον ἀνάξιοι ἐόντες ἴωσι, τοσούτῳ μᾶλλον ἀνακηδεές γίγνονται καί ἀφροσύνη καί θράσεος πίμπλανται " (254).

It would be a great omission if we did not present two more of Democritus' views wherein the concept of political harmony is praised and all forms of civil strife are condemned. He says that it is only through concord that great deeds can be accomplished and that cities can win wars . These goals cannot be achieved in any other way. "᾽Από ὁμονοίας τά μεγάλα ἔργα καί ταῖς πόλεσι τούς πολέμους δυνατόν κατεργάζεσθαι, ἄλλως δι᾽ οὔ" (250). As to civil strife, he similarly points out that it is equally bad for both parties involved as both conqueror and conquered are, to all intents and purposes, destroyed. " Στάσις ἐμφύλιος εἰς ἑκατέρα κακόν · καί γάρ νικέουσι καί ἡττωμένοις ὁμοίη φθορή" (249).

Democritus believed in God. He believed that God has always provided everything for man "πάντα καί πᾶλαι καί νῦν" while man himself creates evil through the blindness of his mind and his lack of judgement. "Διά νοῦ τυφλότητα καί ἀγνωμοσύνην " (175). He also believed in the soul whose benefits are divine whereas those of the body are human and that is why we should prefer the former. As a writer Democritus wrote a multitude of works with peerless skill when compared to Plato.

SOPHISTICAL SCHOOL

The word "Sophist" today has a disparaging meaning. Nevertheless, the Sophists' contribution to intellectual progress was very great and surpasses the contributions of many philosophical schools to the development/evolution of philosophical thought.

Originally the word "Sophist" was applied to a man of experience. Therefore its meaning was not reprehensible. In fact, Aeschylus characterizes the main character of his Prometheus as a Sophist and when he is compared to Zeus he [the Sophist] is called inferior "νωθέστερος". The poet Pindar and the historian Herodotus similarly frequently use the tittle/name of "Sophist", since this was apparently used in place of "philosopher" which was put into use by Socrates and Plato. The fact that the word "Sophist" did not have a bad meaning is evidenced by Aeschines' calling Socrates himself a sophist saying (in his Κατά Τιμάρχου) that the Athenians put the sophist Socrates to death because it was proven that he had been Critias' teacher, and Critias was one of "The Thirty" who had overthrown the democracy. " Ἐπειθ' ὑμεῖς, ὦ ἄνδρες Ἀθηναῖοι, Σωκράτην μέν τόν σοφιστήν ἀπεκτείνατε, ὅτι Κριτίαν ἐφάνη πεπαιδευκώς, ἕνα τῶν τριάκοντα τῶν τόν δήμον καταλυσάντων " (loc. cit. 73).

Sophism had its roots in the desire for the study of human civilization and man himself rather than nature and the universe. It could therefore be called the philosophy of civilization. Of course many manifestations of civilization as, for example, language, religion etc. had been previously studied by philosophers who had preceded the Sophists (Xenophanes, Heraclitus) but their study was done at random and not systematically.

The creation of the world and the discovery of the

primordial being or, in other words, the cosmological and ontological problems seemed insoluble. It was the conflicts between the various philosophical schools and the impossibility of proving one or another correct with proof that led to the development of sophism. As a philosophical trend, sophism caused people to put aside cosmology and matters concerning the nature of being and put forward man either as an individual or as a member of the society he lives in. Here, then, is the basic difference between philosophy and sophism as regards their content. There is also one additional difference as to their aims. Philosophy has the knowledge of truth as its aim; sophism, on the other hand, aims to secure the sovereignity of life. So the former is basically theoretical whereas the latter is highly practical.

The sophists gave paid lessons in the form of lectures on how to be successful in life. The lessons included mathematics, astronomy,grammar (which they completely reformed), the analysis of poetical works from every point of view, music, and, chiefly, rhetoric which they regarded as an all-powerful weapon. All these lessons were necessary to the acquisition of the educational background which would be essential to the service of their cause, which, as we have said, was asserting oneself. The education provided, then, did not aim at the discovery of truth as did the philosophers' education/the education provided by the philosophers, but aimed at providing man with strength so that he would be able to prevail in life.

The Sophists' lectures, given publicly for a fee (in the form of a ticket), had to meet the educational standards of the listeners, otherwise they would not be understood. Because the Sophists spoke before all sorts of audiences they became popularisers of the sciences in order to be understood. Thus they were most valuable to society in that they put before the public the people's moral, social and political problems.

Sophism touched the young deeply. The Sophists were not only excellent teachers but also famous for their inquiries and discoveries in the areas of education and conduct. Plato, for example, who so opposed the Sophists described, in his Protagoras, the enthusiasm and impressions which they inspired in young men not truly with what they said but also how they said it.

These who inexpertly call sophism the negative spectre of philosophy do injustice to the great representatives of the sophistical movement as Protagoras, Gorgias, etc. whose wisdom was shown/proven beyond the shadow of a doubt. In passing we might mention the Sophist Antiphon as an example. In his first work De Veritatis - On Truth he develops his theory as to the conventional formation of the state which Rousseau openly and quite precisely reproduced in Social Contract. Antiphon also distinguished between the laws of the state, which are arbitrarily fixed and the laws of nature, which exist of necessity. " Τά μέν γάρ τῶν νόμων ἐπίθετα, τά δέ τῆς φύσεως ἀναγκαῖα. Antiphon, moreover, declared that time is a measure without an objective basis ". Μέτρον τόν χρόνον, οὐχ ὑπόστασιν".(Aetius). Another Sophist, Prodicus ("wiser than Prodicus" was used for comparison) presented remarkable theories in the field of religion and established synonymy (συνωνυμική) in grammar. Finally, we must mention Hippias who became famous for his studies on the squaring of the circle, the trisection of the angle, etc. and also, Callicles who, in Plato's dialogue

Gorgias, speaks and opposes Socrates. He upheld precisely those theories which Nietzsche presented as his own, that is the supremacy of the strong, the superman (Uebermensch), the social meaning of violence, etc.

Inevitably sophism declined in popularity for its representatives were reduced to quarrelsome distorters of words as were Dionysodorus, Euthydymus, et al. Nevertheless, it is wrong for us to stigmatise the Sophists collectively as perfidious debaters in spite of this being a common belief.

Protagoras (481-411 B.C.)

Protagoras came from Abdera where he was a porter. Diogenes Laertius IX, 53 mentions that Democritus was impressed by the manner in which Protagoras tied some pieces of wood ("ξύλα δεδεκώς") which where to be transported. He later left Abdera and went to different cities teaching people for a fee, "παιδεύειν ἀνθρώποις" Protagoras, 317, B. In Athens he associated with Pericles who assigned him the drawing up of the laws for an Athenian colony in Thurii in Southern Italy. In addition to this he also gave lessons to the sons of the eminent Athenian politician. Also noteworthy is the fact that Euripides was among Protagoras' admirers. According to certain information Protagoras read his books and gave lectures at Euripides' house.

Protagoras taught that truth is relative because everything is constantly developing/evolving. The result of this endless flow is truth's being molded according to our relationship to objects. We remain steadfast in our self-consciousness but reality is not constant therefore constant truth does not exist nor is there a criterion to help us find it. In spite of this, in order for us to have a measure to judge by we ought to take something constant, and this is man. For man recognizes a steadfast existence in himself. Therefore man is the measure of all things: proving to those things which exist that they truly exist, and to those things which do not exist that they do not truly exist. This important phrase, through which the relativity of truth and objectivism are demonstrated, is found in Protagoras' work: Truth or Καταβάλλοντες and is stated as follows: "Πάντων χρημάτων μέτρον ἐστιν ἄνθρωπος τῶν μέν ὄντων ὡς ἔστιν, τῶν δέ μή ὄντων ὡς οὐκ ἔστιν ".Disagreements arose (based on "man is the measure of all things" "πάντων χρημάτων μέτρον ἔστιν ἄνθρωπος") as to what Protagoras meant when he said "man ".Did he take the word as having personal content or did he mean it more broadly? Evidently the opinion prevailed that the term "man" meant a race, made up of related individuals who as related to other races have a special unity which differentiates them and allows them to be presented as one man. This topic has been discussed by Edward Zeller in his History of Greek Philosophy and Theodore Gobertz in his work The Greek Thinkers.-Οἱ Ἕλληνες Στοχασταί.

Man-the individual or race, judges things differently not only in relation to objects, but also to qualities. That which is considered just by A may be considered unjust by B. Or that which A believes to be moral, B believes to be immoral. In conclusion, however, one asks oneself whether Protagoras introduced an individual or a racial objectivism. Racial objectivism seems to have prevailed since the individuals of the same race seem to have the same point of view/position as regards social realities as, for example, justice morality, good, language, customs, etc. Most certainly Protagoras bore this fact in mind when he made his statement for otherwise he would have said that what one Greek judges to be good another finds fault with; good, however, is a general concept recognized by all Greeks to be the same. But the Greek has a different point of view from the Persian and it is from this that racial objectivism arises.

As we have said, the Sophists can be called the philosophers of civilization. Protagoras maintained that civilization arose from man's necessity to preserve himself and to enjoy better conditions of life. As a result, the growth of civilization was contributed to by degrees and after struggles through which man managed to reach higher levels of civilization. In any case he analyzed his views in his work "On the State [of Things] in the Beginning" meaning "on the primitive condition of things" (Περί τῆς ἐν ἀρχῇ καταστάσεως).

As to religion, in his work On Gods-Περί Θεῶν (De Deorum) Protagoras declared that there is no clean proof as to whether gods exist or not. Besides many things which prevent exact knowledge arise. As a result, Protagoras reached the conclusion that he should avoid taking either a negative or positive stand and said that he was not in a position to know if the gods existed or not. "Περί μέν θεῶν οὐκ ἔχω εἰδέναι οὔθ' ὡς οὐκ εἰσίν· πολλά γάρ τα κωλύοντα εἰδέναι...."

Protagoras proved himself a great educator not only in his teaching but also in his teaching methods. He said that in order for education to have results it should reach the degrees of the soul. Teaching, which requires a natural inclination /talent and practice: " Φύσεως καί ἀσκήσεως διδασκαλία δεῖναι"/ Great Word - Μέγας Λόγος should begin at an early age because people should begin learning from their youth. " 'Από νεότητος δέ ἀρξαμένους δεῖ μανθάνειν" Ibid. As may be inferred from the dialogue Protagoras, Protagoras was in favour of a general education for children not for the sake of the acquisition of knowledge but rather for the development of an able personality. Finally, he made a great contribution to the foundation of grammar. It was Protagoras who divided the three genders, determined the tenses and moods of verbs. He studied matters of language in depth and, after scholarly study, discovered two errors in the first verbs of the Iliad. More generally, he believed that language was created by man and is therefore a product of convention and not of nature.

Unfortunately Protagoras' works have not come down to us. Their importance is evidenced by the polemics Plato engaged in in not only his Protagoras but also in his Theaetetus, Euthydemon, Laws, and many works in which he opposed Protagoras' theories or opinions. It is said that in some cases Plato imitated Protagoras. More specifically, Aristoxenos informs us that Protagoras had already written in his Contradictions/Antilogica what Plato said in his Republic. "Πολιτείαν 'Αριστόξενός φησι πᾶσαν σχεδόν ἐν τοῖς Πρωταγόρου γεγράφθαι 'Αντιλογικοῖς". It is likely that in his Contradictions Protagoras concerned himself with matters of public life, justice, etc. In passing we would like to mention that Protagoras considered punishment to be corrective and not vindictive.

Such a person as Protagoras was not easily tolerated by the people because he had the Sophists' tremendous spiritual strength. He was charged with impiety. In order to save his life Protagoras escaped but to his misfortune, the boat which was taking him to Sicily sank and Protagoras was drowned while the Athenians were burning his books.

Gorgias (483-375 B.C.)

Gorgias came from Leontini and was Empedocles' pupil. When he went to Athens to enlist the help of the Athenians against Syracuse he had the opportunity of fighting for the unification of the Greeks against the barbarians.

Politically Gorgias opposed democracy and political equality because he believed that it is not a law of Nature for the stronger to be hindered by the weaker, but rather that the weaker be ruled and led by the stronger and the stronger to give rules which the weaker is to obey. "Πέφυκε γάρ οὐ τό κρεῖσσον ὑπό τοῦ ἥσσονος κωλύεσθαι, ἀλλά τό ἧσσον ὑπό τοῦ κρείσσονος ἄρχεσθαι καί ἄγεσθαι καί τό μέν κρεῖσσον ἡγεῖσθαι, τό δέ ἧσσον ἕπεσθαι" Helen's Encomium (In Praise of Helen) In a way the Sophist Trhasymachus presented the same beliefs for, as Plato says in his Republic, he contended that justice is nothing more than the interest of the stronger. "Φημί δ' ἐγώ εἶναι τό δίκαιον οὐκ ἄλλο τι ἤ τό τοῦ κρείττονος συμφέρον ".

Gorgias communicated the Panhellenic spirit and the desire for the union of all Greeks to conquer the world to Isocrates. Although politically in favour of the unity of the Greeks, that is something positive and of benefit to the nation, philosophically Gorgias could be characterized as an absolute nihilist. He presented his ideas on the subject in his work called On Non-being or On Nature(Περί μή ὄντων ἤ περί φύσεως). It is in this work that one meets the basic tenet of nihilism, this being that being does not exist and if we accept its existence then it cannot be known. Also, if we accept or rather suppose that it can be known then its knowledge cannot be communicated by communication " οὐδέν ἐστιν, εἰ δ' ἐστιν οὐ νοητόν, εἰ δέ νοητόν, ἀλλ' οὐ γνωστόν, εἰ δέ καί γνωστόν, ἀλλ' οὐ δηλωτόν ἄλλοις ". In addition to this, Gorgias argued that being does not exist since, if it did exist, it would have to be either born or unborn. If it were born then it would be subject to decay and therefore it would not be eternal. If it were unborn then, at the same time, it would not be infinite since it would have no beginning. Being infinite it could not be contained in either itself or anything else since either way two beings would exist, that is the place or within which the being would be found, a fact which would refute the existence of one infinite being. In spite of this and if we assume that being exist, Gorgias continued, we cannot come to comprehend it because, if we assume that being exists we logically must conclude that non being does not exist. But, the assumption that non-being does not exist is false. Therefore if the first clause is, of necessity, logically false it follows that the original clause is false. We inevitably reach the conclusion that if we suppose that being exists then it cannot be known and understood. " Οὐκ ἄρα τό ὄν φρονεῖται καί καταλαμβάνεται ".

Finally, as to make being known through communication (assuming that it exists and can be known and understood) this is impossible because we would use words/speech to make this known. But the speech we would use are not beings which truly exist but mere symbols and as a result we would not make beings but rather speech, words known to others. Speech is totally different from beings which exist objectively. " Ὧ γάρ μηνύομεν ἔστι λόγος, λόγος δέ οὐκ ἔστι τά ὑποκείμενα κατά ὄντα οὐκ ἅμα τά ὄντα μηνύομεν τοῖς πέλας ἀλλά λόγον, ὅς ἕτερός ἐστι τῶν ὑποκειμένων" . Nevertheless the acknowledgement of man's inability to come to know beings led Gorgias to a great bore of rhetoric. For Gorgias the purpose of rhetoric is to persuade those who are listening to the speaker, who is called a "psychagogos", that is, a leader of souls.

ATTIC SCHOOL

SOCRATES

Socrates (469-399 B.C.)

Socrates is an immortal hero of philosophy. His life, work and personality have been the hallmark for human thought and deeds throughout the ages. The son of the stone-cutter Sophroniscus and the mid-wife Phaenarete, he was destined to gain everlasting fame.

Socrates' political beliefs were undoubtedly anti-democratic. In fact Zeller, in his History of Greek Philosophy, says that "Socrates made many enemies thanks to his criticism of the democratic form of government." Indeed, it was these very enemies of his who sentenced him to death by a majority of 80 votes. He always thought that we should not listen to the many but to the few and the experts. Besides, whenever he was given the opportunity, Socrates opposed the so-called "will of the people" as, for example, during the trial of the ten generals. He similarly opposed the dictatorship even daring to disobey the orders of the dictatorship of "The Thirty Tyrants" when they ordered the arrest of Leon of Salamis (Λέων ὁ Σαλαμίνιος). Without a doubt Socrates politically at least, supported the aristocracy, that is, the rule of a select few. At the same time he was a brave patriot who fought for his country: he took part in the Potidaea campaign, as well as in the battle at Delium where he showed remarkable courage during the Athenian retreat; he also exhibited great courage in the battle of Amphipolis. His love of country was magnificently rendered by himself in his declaration: "μητρός τε καί πατρός καί τῶν ἄλλων προγόνων ἁπάντων τιμιώτερον ἐστιν ἡ πατρίς καί σεμνότερον καί ἁγιώτερον καί ἐν μείζονι μοίρα καί παρά θεοῖς καί παρ' ἀνθρώποις τοῖς νοῦν ἔχουσι " (Crito).

Unfortunately there is no first-hand information as to what Socrates said because he did no writing himself. We have obtained our information on his teaching from his pupils and especially from Plato.

The basic tenet of the Socratic philosophy is the ascertainment, realization of man's ignorance, the famous " οὐκ εἰδέναι ". "I know only that I know nothing," declared Socrates. It was with this view as his starting point/foundation that Socrates tested everyone who claimed to possess knowledge in whatever they claimed to know.

We must develop a method to test ourselves severely so that we come to know ourselves through self-examination (γνῶθι σαὐτόν). Through self-examination we can also grow to love wisdom and become philosophers for we cannot become wise (σοφοί) ourselves because we are imperfect and finite beings. Only God is wise. Man can only become a philosopher at best. It is through self examination that the moral deed can be achieved. However, occasional intellectual self-examination is not enough. At some point we are obliged to resort to sources of knowledge which are beyond our intellect, that is, a moral introspection dictated by the "daemonium" which determines our conduct. Socrates often mentioned that he heard an inner voice which told him not to do a deed. So, we see that he combined rationality (through his use of definitions, which he introduced into philosophy) and superrationality (in his use of the "daemonium" whenever he could not find a solution to a moral problem through reason). It is to be understood that Socrates' entire system did not aim to settle matters of thought but rather of ethics, meaning practical behaviours.

As we have said, Socrates started out with his "οὐκ εἰδέναι". Socrates "did not know" and came into contact with people who claimed to know. For example, the general Laches "knew" what bravery is. Socrates would approach him and begin a discussion on the nature of bravery with him. In the end it would be proven that the general thought he knew whereas in reality he did not know. He would fall into contradictions and so be forced to admit ignorance. Thus we come to the famous Socrates irony "through which Socrates would hide that which he revealed and at the same time would reveal that which he hid. Through this "irony" Socrates would uncover ignorance and bring it into the open. In exposing the ignorance of the person he was talking/speaking with, Socrates seemed to be ironical; his irony, however, was a system, a means by which to seek the truth and certainly not meant to tease.

Once man is rid of his delusions and becomes aware of his imperfection, he feels the need to strive for his perfection at the same time. He ardently desires to leave the truth and so "eros" is born within him Eros, therefore is a necessity or rather a tendency of the soul to attain perfection. It is a bridge joining the imperfect man with the perfect God. It is a great daemon found in the space between man and God "μεταξύ ἐστι Θεοῦ τε καί θνητοῦ ". (Symposium, 202 E). Through eros the soul is elevated or tends to elevate itself to perfection that is, the divine. In other words as a force eros gives man strength and guides him in his conception of truth. Therefore eros is of value to education/has educational value and it is for this reason that Socrates tried to excite man's latent desire to search for truth. He especially addressed himself to young men because, as he said, they are like the green branches of trees which are easily bent and so grow in the direction we desire. On the other hand, when a tree is full grown its hard branches cannot be bent; they are like old people.

We have mentioned the verb "to know" and we ought to explain that knowledge, as conceived by Socrates, does not mean the mere comprehension of a concept but also its application in one's way of life. This means that a knowledge of philanthropy does not mean an intellectual perception of the term "philanthropy" but rather a practical application of the essence of philanthropy. As a result, knowledge is not only an act involving the intellect but one also involving the will and the senses and which manifests itself in ones social behaviour. It may be inferred from the above that Socrates did not found a theoretical school; he fought for the moral improvement of man and this moreover, was his life's purpose. He also believed that no one is bad of his own volition ("οὐδείς ἑκών κακός") and that man can become good (agathos) through knowledge.

As to religion, Socrates accepted the existence of a God who is truly wise ("τῷ ὄντι ὁ Θεός σοφός εἶναι" Apology) and immortal. He himself was very devout and the charges that he did not believe in the gods of the state were completely groundless. At the same time he believed in the immortality of the soul hence the intimation in the Apology wherein he said that the time had come for him to die and for the rest to live but only God knew who would be going to the better place " ἀλλά γάρ ἤδη ὥρα ἀπιέναι, ἐμοί μέν ἀποθανουμένῳ, ὑμῖν δέ βιωσομένοις· ὁπότεροι δέ ἡμῶν ἔρχονται ἐπ' ἄμεινον πρᾶγμα, ἄδηλον παντί πλήν θεῷ ".

While imprisoned, Socrates retained his familiar serenity and occupied himself with making up poems and versifying Aesop's fables. Finally, before drinking the hemlock, he gave an excellent lecture full of moral content and which is presented by Plato in his Phaedo. "Καί δεθείς μετ' οὐ πολλάς ἡμέρας ἔπιε τό κώνειον πολλά καλά καί ἀγαθά διαλεχθείς, ἅ Πλάτων ἐν τῷ Φαίδωνι φησίν". (Diogenes Laertius, XI, 42).

Describing Socrates' last moments in his Phaedo Plato says "... and my tears poured forth of their own, like a river so that when I had covered my face I gave myself up to lamenting not him but myself for losing such a friend... Apollodorus had continually tears in his eyes from before and then (as soon as Socrates had drunk the hemlock) broke everyone's heart with his lamenting and show of indignation including a great bellow. Only Socrates remained unmoved. He said. "What are these things that you are doing you strange people? I sent the women away precisely because I wanted to avoid such discord ".

Socrates last words were the following. "O Crito we owe Asclepius a cock. Keep this promise and do not neglect it "."This will be done," Crito answered, "however, see if you want to say anything else." Socrates did not respond to this. "Ὦ Κρίτων, τῷ Ἀσκληπιῷ ὀφείλομεν ἀλεκτρύονα· ἀλλ' ἀπόδοτε καί μή ἀμελήσητε. Ἀλλά ταῦτα, ἔφη, ἔσται ὁ Κρίτων, ἀλλ' ὅρα εἴ τι ἄλλο λέγεις. Ταῦτα ἐρομένου αὐτοῦ, οὐδέν ἔτι ἀπεκρίνατο..."

MEGAREAN SCHOOL

Euclid (450-380 B.C.)

Euclid came from Megara. He was one of Socrates' oldest pupils. He risked his life a number of times so that he might be able to listen to Socrates teach: during the Peloponesian War he often went to Athens disguised as a woman for his hometown of Megara was at war with Athens. This is reliable information handed down to us by the Roman writer and friend of Herodes Atticus, Aulus Gellius who cites this in his Attic Nights. It seems that Euclid was a close friend of Plato and that after Socrates had been put to death (a scene also witnessed by Euclid) Plato and the other pupils of the dead philosopher went to Megara to be with him.

Euclid had investigated the teachings of the Eleatics and more especially Parmenides and they influenced him to such a degree that he formulated and supported truly Eleatic views on being, movement and decay. Euclid stated that the being is unique and anything differing from it does not exist. Nothing which is born moves or decays exists. "Τό ὄν ἕν εἶναι καί τό ἕτερον μή εἶναι μηδέ γεννᾶσθαι τι μηδέ φθείρεσθαι το παράπαν". The above fragment has been handed down to us by Eusebius in his Proparaskeve Euangeliu (Preparation of the Gospel) (14,7) as having been said by Euclid according to Aristocles of Messenia. We are obliged to use "second-hand" sources to learn Euclides' views because not even fragments of the famous dialogues he wrote have reached use. The only thing we know of them are their names which are cited by Diogenes Laertius.

Euclid was influenced by Socrates as well as the Eleatics. Perhaps this explains why he considered that the unique being which was the creation of Eleatics was identical to the good of the Socratic philosophy. He maintained that the Good is the same as the one being which exists and which is called by various names: sometimes prudence, sometimes good, and sometimes mind. "Οὗτος ἕν τό ἀγαθόν ἀπεφαίνετο πολλοῖς ὀνόμασι καλούμενον ὁτέ μέν γάρ φρόνησιν, ὁτέ δέ θεόν καί ἄλλοτε νοῦν καί τά λοιπά". (Diog. Laert. II). Also noteworthy is Euclid's view that all things which are in opposition to the Good do not exist. "Τά δέ ἀντικείμενα τῷ ἀγαθῷ ἀνήρει μή εἶναι φάσκων".(Ibid.) The whole of philosophy of contemporary biology is hidden in the aforementioned opinion. This includes Darwinism. It is held that any thing which contributes to make existence whole is moral. In other words for Euclid God was being and so Evil was non being. Therefore the supporters of biological philosophy by analogy maintain that whatever promotes existence is good whereas whatever harms it is evil. So Augustine, who similarly declared that evil is the lack of good, did nothing more than to repeat Euclid's opinion in another way. Gobertz compared Euclid to Augustine on the subject in his treatise on the Greek thinkers.

Euclid's school was called eristic because the discussion often took such a vehement turn that the name eristic was justified. As a matter of fact, unfavourable comments on Euclid were caused by the acerbity of the dialogues. Euclid was accused of planting the madness for contentious discussion in the hearts of the Megareans. "Μεγαρεῦσιν ὅς ἔμβαλε λύσσαν ἐρισμοῦ" (Timon). The accusations were, of course, exaggerated; nevertheless, it is true that the Megarean School, especially as exemplified by Euclid's pupil and Demosthene's teacher Eubulides, presented the most sophisms (deliberate wrong reasoning) fallacies. As Eubulides asked, in "The Bald man" (" Ὁ Φαλακρός"), "Does one become bald by one hair?" "No." was the answer. "By two hairs?" "No." "By three?" "No". Finally, when an affirmative answer is given, as it must be at some point, we reach the conclusion that one becomes bald by even one hair. Euclides, who came from Miletus, bitterly opposed Aristotle against whom he even wrote a book. To fight sophisms Aristotle wrote his work Sophistical Controls /Controlling Sophisms /Keeping Sophism in Check-Σοφιστικοί Ἔλεγχοι in which he recommends methods of disproving sophism through/by means of proper checking.

In spite of all these Euclid was famous for the decency of his character as well as his disposition. In his Moralia - Ἠθικά (moral essay) Plutarch mentions the following anecdote. When, after an argument, Euclid's brother said to him, "I wish I might perish if I do not punish you" Euclid answered, "I, too, wish to be destroyed if I do not convince you ". The result was that his brother repented. "Ἀπολοίμην εἰ μή σε τιμωρησαίμην, ἐγώ δέ, φήσας, ἀπολοίμην εἰ μή σε πείσαιμι ".

Stilpon (380-300 B.C.)

Stilpon came from Megara. He became famous for his ability to find arguments to support his contentions and to disprove all that he himself denied. This ability of his brought glory to the Megarean school which some reknown philosophers joined after abandoning other schools. Zeno, the founder of Stoicism, for example, was one of Stilpon's pupils.

Stilpon's philosophy, especially in the area of ethics, was influenced by the Cynic Diogenes whose pupil Stilpon was. Thus he accepted spiritual goods as most important, always placing them above sensual ones. He was also influenced by the Eleatics for he taught that the being is unique, indivisible, unborn and immortal. He moreover rejected every belief as regards motion. For Stilpon the verb "to become" was non-existent. he similarly rejected Plato's theory of Ideas. In fact, he would say that the cabbage presented to us is not a cabbage because the ideal cabbage is that which has existed from eternity and as a result is not the one we now have before us which therefore is not a cabbage."Οὐδ' ἄρα τοῦδε τό λάχανον οὐκ ἔστι τό δεικνυόμενον λάχανον γάρ ἦν πρό μυρίων ἐτῶν οὐκ ἄρα ἐστί τοῦτο λάχανον ".The above reasoning is based on the thought that if we accept that the ideal cabbage exists those objects which we perceive by the senses and which we call cabbages are not real cabbages because it is not possible for an object to be both ideal and perceptible to/by the senses.

Stilpon also introduced a novelty in logic by declaring that we cannot assign to a subject a predicate other than the subject itself. That is to say, the sentence

"The horse is beautiful" is not correct because we identify beauty with the horse, and they are two different things. The correct judgment is "The horse is a horse". He nevertheless believed that true knowledge depended on logic.

Diogenes Laertius (B, 114) wrote a number of things about Stilpon's eristic genius through which he managed to dazzle Greece to such a degree that little was needed (" ὥστε μικροῦ δεῆσαι") for "πᾶσαν τήν Ἑλλάδα ἀφορῶσαν εἰς αὐτόν μεγαρίσαι ". In spite of this his great ability in dialectic was not able to rescue him from the Council (Boule) of the Athenians who banished him from their city.

Another famous member of the Megarean was Diodorus Cronus/Kronos (Διόδωρος ὁ Κρόνος) who opposed Aristotle's philosophy on that which might exist (περί " δυνάμει ὄντος") and that which now exists (ἐνεργείᾳ ὄντος) with the argument (which was called "κυριεύων" meaning irrefutable) that only that which is real is possible: "δυνατόν εἶναι μόνον τό πραγματικόν". This argument, mentioned by Arrian in his "Ἐπικτήτου διατριβαί " (Epictitus' Treatises/Discourses) , together with the notes accompanying it in this text, inspired the German philosopher Nikolai Hartmann to write his book Potential and Reality(Δυνατότης καί Πραγμάτικότης). Diodorus came to a tragic end. Finding himself at a banquet Stilpon asked him some dialectical questions before King Ptolemy Soter (Ptolemy I). "Λόγους, τινάς διαλεκτικούς ἠρωτήθη." Being unable to give satisfactory answers he was derided by the King who called him Cronus/ Kronos. Extremely dejected, Diodorus left the banquet. After writing a book giving the answers to

Stilpon's questions he died of melancholy. "᾽Αθυμία τόν βίον κατέστρεψεν", as Diogenes Laertius reports.

Finally, we must mention Alexinus, a pupil of Stilpon's who, because of his passion for disputation was called "Elenxinus" (᾽Ελεγξῖνος) (from the noun ἔλεγξις meaning refutation). He wrote a whole book against Aristotle as well as a treatise Peri Agoges - Περί ᾽Αγωγῆς (On Behaviour) a fragment of which was recently found.

ELIOERETRIAN SCHOOL

Phaedo (5th/4th cent. B.C.)

We know very little about Phaedo's philosophy. As we may conclude from the few remnants of his works which are extant, he believed that one attains true freedom and rids himself of passions of the soul through philosophy. Unfortunately the dialogues he wrote have not survived. This is a great loss, because as was generally admitted, Phaedo was Socrates' favourite pupil so he must have been intelligent and not in the least inferior to Socrates' other, more reknown, pupils. In any case, we are told that he was a brave patriot, having fought against the Spartans in the war between Elis (Ἠλεία [mod. Gk], Ἠλίς [anc. Gk]) and Sparta. He was captured but released thanks to a ransom gathered at Socrates' request. Phaedo founded his own school in Elis (Ἠλίς), the Elian Socratic school, and taught there successfully. Nevertheless, he was introduced into history and became very famous thanks to Plato's homonymous dialogue wherein Phaedo exposes Socrates' ideas on the immortality of the soul, presented during his last moments in his cell where Phaedo was present, to Phliasius Echecrates, a Pythagorian. Little else is known about Phaedo.

Menedemus (350-278 B.C.)

Menedemus came from Eretria. he loved his home town so much that he died "extremely grieved by its misfortune" (Zeller, History of the Greek Philosophy). He was descended from an aristocratic family, however he worked as both a builder and tent-maker. He had the opportunity to occupy himself with philosophy when he found himself at Megara with a military detachment. He heard Stilpon and Phaedo teach and founded his own school on his return to Eretria. Unfortunately the information concerning his philosophy is so indefinite or contradictory that we cannot even guess what he believed. It seems, however, that he accepted the Eleatics' view on the unity of the being; at the same time, Diogenes Laertius has maintained the impression that he/they denied the identity of that which is good and that which is beneficial. Simplicius also provided the information that Menedemus' pupils "refuted qualities" ("ἀνήρουν τάς ποιότητας"), meaning that he did not acknowledge the existence of qualities because they lack a common essential substance but rather exist in the specific things perceived by each of us. Menedemus also participated in politics for the benefit of his home town. He was sent by the Eretrians as a representative to Demetrius Poliorcetes, Ptolemy and Lysimachus . In the end, however his countrymen, incited by the democrats, persecuted him. He managed to escape by taking refuge in a temple. He later ended up in the court of his friend Antigonus Gonatas where he later commited suicide without having put down his ideas in books.

CYNIC SCHOOL

DIOGENES “THE DOG”

Antisthenes (445-365 B.C.)

Antisthenes, who was born in Athens, was originally a pupil of Gorgias. Because of a disagreement, however, he abandoned Gorgias after having insulted him. Afterwards, evidently impressed by his exemplary life, he followed Socrates as both pupil and admirer. As a matter of fact he was present at the philosopher's last hours in prison.

After Socrates' death, Antisthenes founded his own philosophical school which he located somewhere near Cynosargus thus giving rise to the name "cynic" as applied to his supporters. Another explanation for the name "cynic" is that it comes from the carefree attitude which distinguished them as well as their wandering life. Antisthenes himself proudly carried the nickname "Haplocyon" "Ἁπλοκύων" meaning genuine dog.

Antisthenes was a clever rhetor and presented his ideas in an extremely convincing manner. At the same time he did not neglect to be excessively biting and witty in his sarcastic replies. Once, when he was asked whether it is better to marry a beautiful or ugly woman, he answered that in marrying a beautiful woman one has a common one ("κοινή") while in marrying an ugly one one has a sentence ("ποινή"=punishment). He held Plato in contempt because he busied himself with many theoretical lessons and diverted his attention from the practical value of life.

Antisthenes considered the shaking off of a bad as well as the use of few words as necessary lessons. "Ἐρωτηθείς τί τῶν μαθημάτων ἀναγκαιότατον, ἔφη, τό κακά ἀπομαθεῖν ". (Diog. Laert.) He called Plato "Satho ".

But once, when he was mocking the theories on Ideas (Forms) saying that he was able to see the horse, but unable to see the idea (form) of the horse, Plato answered him saying, "you have the eye (meaning the sensuous one) with which to see the horse but you haven't managed to acquire the eye (meaning the intellectual one) with which to see the form (idea) of the horse ". "῞Ιππον μέν ὁρῶ, ἱππότητα δέ οὐχ ὁρῶ. Καί ὅς εἶπεν, ἔχεις μέν ᾧ ἵππος ὁρᾶται τόδε τό ὄμμα, ᾧ δέ ἱππότης θεωρεῖται οὐδέπω κέκτησαι". Elsewhere Plato, turning against Antisthenes, calls him an old man educated late . (Sophist, 251 B).

Regardless of Antisthenes' teasing and recrimination which struck even Isocrates and Alcibiades, the Cynic philosophy presented many noteworthy findings. First of all, the aim set for philosophy was not theoretical but rather moral knowledge, meaning man's behaviour. Knowledge is of value as long as it contributes to the attainment of virtue (arete) which alone leads man to true happiness. The ideal of life is living by virtue ("κατ' ἀρετήν ζῆν"). Virtue is something that can be taught. ("'Αρετήν διδακτήν εἶναι"). One does not need theories and discussions nor does one need to subjugate to laws in order to attain virtue. One need only allow one's nature to develop itself freely, completely free of bonds and of external obligations or self-delusions. In order to achieve this we must live naturally so that we might offset the various obligations which we and not nature created for ourselves. In this manner we cease to be depended upon happenings in the outside world. In order to achieve/attain happiness a philosopher must accustom himself to want, hardship and frugality. Faithful to his beliefs, Antisthenes had no house or other property and wandered about barefoot, in an old tribon (a cheap mantle) carrying a stick. He considered the study of the meanings of words so important that he thought his study the basic condition for all education. " Ἀρχή παιδεύσεως ἡ τῶν ὀνομάτων ἐπίσκεψις ". (This opinion of Antisthenes may be found in Epictitus' Treatises/Discourses).

Antisthenes, moreover, denied the existence of general meanings and believed that contradiction was logically impossible since each word represents only one and the same thing. If we use the same word in the discussion contradiction is inconceivable since, as we said before, we indicate the same thing by/through/with the same word. If on the other hand, we do not mean the same thing then we are talking about different things. So, if the one speaker is talking about one thing and the other speaker about another then a discussion cannot develop nor, consenquently, can a contradiction arise. Thus we are led to the conclusion that when people disagree they are not talking about the same thing. Antisthenes proclaimed primitive sensationalist views when he declared that that which we perceive through our senses corresponds to the truth.

As to his political beliefs, Antisthenes was anti-democratic. In fact he believed that the laws were made for the many and not for the few elite who are guided by arete (virtue). In any case he did not concern himself with politics. As to his religious beliefs, he did not accept the existence of many gods, as most people thought, but rather believed in one God because only one exists by nature. "Κατά νόμον εἶναι πολλούς θεούς, κατά δε φύσιν ἕνα ".

Antisthenes presented his views in works which covered a total of ten large volumes; however, none of them is extant.

Diogenes "the Dog" (404-323 B.C.)

Diogenes, nicknamed "the Dog" ("other dogs bite their enemies; I my friends in order to correct them") was born in Sinope on the Black Sea but was banished and went to Athens at an early age. Once in Athens he declared, "I have sentenced the inhabitants of Sinope to remain there." As a pupil of Antisthenes he came to know and espouse the Cynic philosophy, to which he added sarcasm.

Diogenes believed that man is created by nature in such a way as to be able to cope with the needs of life. In spite of this, man created for himself various appetites, desires for goods, and, in general, created a great number of artificial needs. In the end, these artificial needs enslave him, destroy his peace of mind (ψυχική γαλήνη) and do away with the independence of his personality. Faithful to his belief Diogenes lived exactly (if not to an extreme degree) as he believed in theory. He walked around barefoot, wearing a cheap tunic (chiton) and brandishing a long stick. At night he would usually sleep in a large earthen jar (πίθος) near the Acropolis. During the day he would go around the city strictly checking and mocking all the bad things about the city, especially the antisocial elements. We cite two examples. Once, when he saw the phrase "Μηδέν εἰσίτω κακόν" ("Let not evil enter here"), written above the door of a corrupt man, he knocked at the door and asked, "Where does the owner of the house enter from?" On another occasion when he saw the adulterous doctor Didymus examining a young girl Diogenes remarked to him, "Be careful that you do not seduce the apple of her father's eye while treating her eye ". ("Πρόσεξε μήπως θεραπεύων τόν ὀφθαλμόν, διαφθείρεις τήν κόρην")*.

Diogenes' boldness and criticism provoked the anger of those who bore the brunt of his sarcasm. They did him no harm, nevertheless, and Diogenes became more and more provocative with his spiteful observations. While on his way to Aegina he was seized by pirates and taken to Crete where he was sold into bondage. When asked what kind of work he could do he answered, " Ἀνθρώπων ἄρχειν ". ("Lead men"). Diogenes was bought as a slave by the Corinthian Xeniades. Xeniades held him in such esteem that he assigned Diogenes his children's upbringing. From Corinth Diogenes often went to Athens where he talked with various philosophers, more especially with Plato. It seems that there grew a mutual admiration between the two men. Plato would call him "the raging Socrates" and would make sure to return the bitter comments the Cynic made. The following incident is typical. Once, on entering Plato's opulent household, Diogenes pompously stepped on the magnificent carpets barefoot saying." I am walking on Plato's vanity ". "True," Plato replied, "but with another vanity ".

Diogenes believed that man was created in God's image but later fell. In order to become what he was and to reach the highest moral standard which suits him, a complete reformation of man and society is necessary. Diogenes felt that it was his duty to reform or transform "men" in men. He preformed his duty with perseverance and surprising intelligence completely ignoring the dangers involved. In fact, in order to stress the lack of honest men Diogenes wandered about with the famous lantern in his hand muttering, "Ἄνθρωπον ζητῶ ". ("I am looking for an honest man "). Diogenes also wrote a number of books which however, are not extant. He had no family and many people accused him of being unpatriotic. Diogenes was a Greek and felt himself to be a citizen of the cosmopolis of Greece. His country was to be found everywhere in Greece and, whenever called upon to do so, he fought for it. The Stoic Dionysius tells us that Diogenes took part in the Battle of Chaeronia and was captured. He was then presented to Philip who asked, "Who are you?" "Someone to spy on your greed," was the Cynic's response. Philip stood up, looked closely at him and then ordered him freed. Diogenes showed his desire to fight for his country yet another time. As a slave he did not have the right to bear arms. So, when the Corinthians were getting ready for an imminent enemy attack, Diogenes ceaselessly rolled his storage jar from here to there. Asked why he was doing that he shouted, "I am ashamed to sit around doing nothing when everyone else is working so hard.

Diogenes was a believer in aristocracy. (In fact, he once had a slave. When his slave ran away Diogenes was advised to go after him to which he replied, "It would be ridiculous for Manes to be able to manage without Diogenes and Diogenes not to be able to manage without Manes "). He believed in the superiority of spirit and the justice (he once shouted to a paunchy orator, struggle [to accomplish his mission]. He taught social "Anaximenes, give some belly to the poor") and believed in endeavour as a moral principle of life. (As an old man he refused to rest saying, "If I were a runner on the track would it be right for me to abandon the competition a bit before the end or would I have to make an even greatest effort ? ").

Diogenes had an intense personality which he refused to modify. As a slave he had declared, "captive lions are not the slaves of the man who feeds them, but rather the man their slave ". Even when the all-powerful Alexander asked to see him, Diogenes did not go. "I do not want to see him. If he wants to see me let him come ". When Alexander went and stood before his jar, he asked. " What do you want me to do for you, Diogenes?" "To move so you don't hide the sun from me ". Alexander moved aside whispering, "If I weren't Alexander I would like to be Diogenes ". Alexander and Diogenes died the same day. The one in Babylon of a serious illness and the other in Corinth holding his breath of his own volition.

Another famous Cynic was Crates of Thebes who, after donating all his property (300 talents) to his country set off to wander with only a stick and a satchel. He was called "Door-Opener"("θυρεπανοίκτης") because he had the ability to inspire confidence so that doors opened for him. In his wanderings he was accompanied by his wife, Hipparchia, and her brother, Metrocles, who originated the "Chria" (Χρεία), a literary form related to the narration of humorous stories.

The following important Cynics lived during the Hellenistic period. Bion, a former slave who wrote many books full of puns and irony for which he was accused of "dressing philosophy up in the motley clothes of a hetaera ". Menippus, a former slave who became Metrocles' pupil and ended up with absolute satire, thus originating Menippean Satire. Meleager, another satirical poet. Phoenix of Colophon who provided new impetus for the "choliambus" (χολίαμβος). Poseidippus, the epigram writer. Teles, the writer of serious works.

HEDONIST SCHOOL

Aristippus (435-355 B.C.)

Aristippus was descended from a wealthy family that lived in Cyrene. Once, when he had gone to Olympia for the Games, he was told of Socrates' teachings. He grew so enthusiastic about them that he decided to remain in Athens and become his pupil. So he installed himself in Athens and, although he followed Socrates' lectures, he refused to conform with his moral teachings since he preferred to enjoy the pleasures of a voluptuous life. He was criticized for not interrupting his indolent life in order to be with Socrates at his last moments since he, too, was in Aegina then. The truth is that he did not want to go to the prison not out of indifference or so as not to interrupt his enjoyment but so that he would not betray his theories on pleasure (hedone). If he had gone to be with Socrates at his last moments this would have brought him great sadness a sentiment which he was obliged to avoid thanks to his philosophical beliefs. After Socrates' death he returned to Cyrene where he established his own school and taught most successfully.

One of Aristippus' fundamental beliefs was the well-known "ἔχω καί οὐκ ἔχομαι ". ("I own but I am not owned"). According to his principle, which implies man's sovereignity over things and circumstances and not vice versa, we can be led to freedom from within, which is the purpose of philosophy. Nevertheless, Aristippus considered the gratification of one's senses as life's purpose and that is precisely why he devoted himself to the enjoyment of pleasures seeking to please himself with pleasures of the present. For, as he himself said, memories of past pleasures or anticipation of future pleasure are not related to ourselves because, on the one hand, the past no longer exists and, on the other, the future is beyond the existing present." Τό δέ ἀπολελαυκέναι καί ἀπολαύσειν οὐδέν νομίζων πρός αὐτόν, τό μέν οὐκ ἐτ' ὄν τό δέ ὡς οὔπω ". (Athenaeus, Deipnosophistae, 544). Once the present had been given such priority, Aristippus concluded that present pleasure is good. This present pleasure is called "monochronius" that is, specific present pleasure, and "a state of the body" since carnal pleasure is far superior to the pleasure of the soul. "Πολύ μέντοι τῶν ψυχικῶν τάς σωματικάς ἀμείνους εἶναι ". (Diogenes Laertius, XI, 9).

Aristippus taught that the seeking of pleasure is a general phenomenon and rule of life to be found not only in man but even among animals. Man should therefore use his good sense to weigh things so that he might choose those things which give him pleasure thus satisfying his natural inclination to it (pleasure). It should be noted, however, that the pleasure of Aristippus is different from that of Epicurus. The former tended to a positive pleasure resulting from motion, maintaining that the absence of sadness is not pleasure. The latter considered as pleasure that state which does not result from motion but from peace and quiet.

Epistemologically the Cyrenaics taught that man can, perceive subjective states only. When we cut ourselves, they said, we come to know the suffering of the cut and not if that which has cut us is iron or something else. This is true when we burn ourselves. "Καιόμενοι γάρ ἔλεγον ἤ τεμνόμενοι, γνωρίζομεν ὅτι πάσχομεν τι.Πότερον δέ τό καῖον εἴη πῦρ ἤ τό τέμνον σίδηρος οὐκ ἔχειν εἰπεῖν" . (Ibid).If the above view is introduced, and man knows only his own subjective states, then it necessarily follows that moral ideals do not exist objectively but arise from convention. Therefore nothing is just or good or shameful by nature; but these come to exist by custom or agreement. "Μηδέν εἶναι φύσει δίκαιον ἤ καλόν ἤ αἰσχρόν, ἀλλά νόμῳ καί ἔθει". (Ibid).

Among Aristippus' pupils was his daughter Arete who, in turn introduced her son, Aristippus to his grandfather's teachings. Aristippus the grandson called "metrodidactus" (mother taught"), expressed the view that we can distinguish three states, related to our sensuous moods. In the first we feel sadness, which is like the rough sea:"τῷ κατά θάλασσαν χειμῶνι". In the second we feel pleasure which is like the gentle waves.("Τῷ λείῳ κύματι"). Finally, in the third we feel neither sadness nor pleasure. This state is the same as peace. ("Γαλήνη παραπλησίαν οὖσαν"). This theory of the younger Aristippus, according to which our sensuous moods are interpreted by involuntary motions has been reproduced by today's supporters of natural psychology.

Theodorus was another famous Cyrenaic. He taught that the laws should be in effect for the masses while superior people, such as the sophoi (wise men) should not be obliged to obey them. Other Cyrenaics were: Amniceris (who accepted sacrifice for the sake of one's country even though he was a Hedonist), Antipatrus of Cyrene (who had many pupils) and many others whose works together with those of the founder of the Schools, are not extant.

Hegesias (3rd century B.C.)

Hegesias who lived in the third century B.C., taught in Alexandria during the reign of Ptolemy I. He had been a pupil of the Cyrenaic Paraebates*. Hegesias' theory lay in the realization that happiness is utterly unattainable. This is so because the body is full of many sufferings, the soul is troubled by emotions because it suffers along with the body, and to top this all off, fate hinders the realization of all the good things man hopes for: "Τήν εὐδαιμονίαν ὅλως ἀδύνατον εἶναι· τό μέν γάρ σῶμα πολλῶν ἀναπεπλῆσθαι παθημάτων τήν δέ ψυχήν συμπαθεῖν τῷ σώματι καί ταράττεσθαι, τήν δέ τύχην πολλά τῶν κατ' ἐλπίδα κωλύειν". (Diogenes Laertius, XI, 94). Hegesias, according to reliable information handed down to us by Cicero (Tusc. I, 84), wrote a book which was, unfortunately, lost. In this book a man attempting to commit suicide by starvation describes the tragedy of life and the misfortunes it is full of. The title of the book was as pessimistic as its contents, the title being Apokarteron ("The disheartened One"), that is, a man who can no longer bear life.

Hegesias was a Hedonist. How can Hedonism reconcile itself with the desire for death which is characteristic of him? It may be reconciled through the following reasoning. Pleasure is proven to be unattainable. The only thing that exists in life is pain. The wise man therefore ought not to seek that which is pleasant and does not exist but rather to avoid that which is unpleasant and does exist. Thus, if happiness is positively unattainable then we ought to seek it negatively, by avoiding pain, so that we will be led to the psychological state of happiness through "painlessness". Unfortunately, it is more or less impossible to avoid sadness as long as we live, so we will not have a state of "painlessness"; this "painlessness" is attainable only after death. Since death frees us from pain the final conclusion of Hegesias' argument logically is, "Commit suicide ". It seems that his teaching was successful for, on the one hand, he acquired the nickname "Pisithanatus" (Πεισιθάνατος) ("Death Convincer") and, on the other, Ptolemy forbade his teaching in order to put a stop to the wave of suicides which Hegesias' lectures gave rise to. As to relations among people, Hegesias suggested doing away with hatred and showing more understanding of human fault, which arise from human passions. Arthur Schopenhauer borrowed Hegesias' pessimistic thought.

ACADEMIC SCHOOL
OR
THE ACADEMY

PLATO

Plato (427-348 B.C.)

Undoubtedly Plato (whose real name was Aristocles, and who was given the name Plato [Πλάτων] [from the adjective πλατύς "broad"] because of his broad forehead, was the most important of Socrates' pupils. He was a true giant of universal thought, it bearing the indelible mark of his wisdom.

Plato was descended from an aristocratic family when ancestors went back to Codrus and Solon. Plato applied himself to politics both because of a natural inclination and his ancestry. Basically he was as much against dictatorship as democracy. He presented his fundamental beliefs in his famous work, Republic, wherein he describes a form of government which is clearly antidemocratic.

Political society, which is founded by natural necessity (φυσική ἀνάγκη) is divided into three classes. 1)The archontes-ἄρχοντες ("leaders", "rulers") who are to have political power and who are to be educated people who know how to philosophize about life. 2) The phylakes-φύλακες ("guards") who are to look after the republic's safety and enforce the decisions of the archontes and who are to come from the ranks of courageous citizens. 3) The farmers and craftsmen who, guided by the archontes and protected by the phylakes, are to secure society's material well-being by means of their work.

From the above it may be concluded that Plato took the three parts of the human soul as a measure of division for society: 1) the logistic (λογιστικόν) part which corresponds to the archontes, 2) the bold (θυμοειδές) part which corresponds to the phylakes, and 3) the desirous (ἐπιθυμητικόν) part which corresponds to the makers. Let us not forget that Plato established the principle of eugenics, granting the archontes the right to arrange marriages for the sake of improving the quality of the community of citizens.

The fact that in the Republic Plato declares that the first two classes are not to have personal property or families gave rise to some people's believing that he introduced a Communist form of government. This is totally wrong. On the one hand, Plato distinguishes social classes according to merit regardless of economic status and wants classes to exist. Communism, on the other hand, desires the abolition of classes and the establishment of a classless society. In his old age Plato returned to the scientific study of political society and published his Laws (Nomoi) wherein he: acknowledges that all citizens have the right to own property, legally safeguards the functions of the state, takes measures against the ungodly, accepts slavery, and, in general, once again supports antidemocratic views. We must, in any case, note that Plato sets the achievement of Good as the purpose of the state. This is achieved when the citizens become virtuous by means of the proper education. And now we come to the famous idea of the Good about which so much has been written by people who have especially studied Plato and about which Plato himself wrote so little. In the Republic Plato likens the idea of Good with the Sun which gives objects their genesis and visibility without itself belonging to the area of genesis, etc. Thus the idea of Good gives objects their knowledge and substance, without Good being substance but rather above and beyond it. As a result, when Plato speaks of Good, he does not understand it to be a moralistic concept but rather a dynamic-ὑπερβατικήν principle, capable of giving to objects existence and then knowledge about themselves. So, the achievement of Good means the materialization of the dynamic principle which can give to a society its existence. In other words, Plato sets the preservation and advancement of society as the goals of the state. Let us not forget that the word agathos in ancient Greek implied one who is full of strength, courage and vitality. Consequently the achievement of Good in civil reality cannot but express the pursuit of strength and vitality in society. This selfsame concept of the Good can, according to Plato, be attained by virtuous citizens that is, citizens who are distinguished by justice, wisdom, courage and common sense.

Plato, nevertheless, became famous for his teachings on Ideas (or Forms). He was the first to use the term "idea" but with a different meaning from today. When we speak of an idea today we mean an objective concept whereas Plato meant an ontological state which existed objectively, That is, Plato accepted the sensuous and conceptional world. The sensuous world is the world of genesis and decay, the world of constant change that we live and move in. Beyond this world there is another superior and perfect world, which makes up ideal reality.The world of ideas, not being subject to decay, is eternal and, naturally, constant. Nevertheless, at the same time there exists a dialectic relationship of similarity and contrast between the two worlds. The similarity lies in that the sensuous world is an imitation of the conceptual world; that is, it was created with the conceptual world as its model. The conceptual world is the eternal archetype of perceptible objects to which it gives shape.

The classic example of the analysis of the relationship between the conceptual and sensuous world is the seal. We can reproduce the same image thousands of times in clay with the same seal. However, the image cut into the seal happens to be the unique original model. This is also true of Ideas (Forms). They are the ones which originally exist and it is from them that perceptible beings receive their shape without the Ideas losing their independent existence. Thus every being of the perceptible world has been created with an Idea as its model. Ideas (Forms) as a whole make up what Plato calls the "beings of being ". Consequently, as a result of all that has been said, there is a relationship of similarity between conceptual and perceptible reality. At the same time there is a relationship of contrast which precisely lies in this: the one is eternal and constant and the other subject to decay and transient.

Another point which should be made clear is Plato's dialectic compared with that of Zeno. Aristotle considered Zeno the Eleatic as the originator of dialectic. However Zeno's dialectic differed from Plato's in that Zeno showed the contradictions and opposite views of things in order to prove a statement false whereas Plato, in his dialectic, sought the morphological varieties of objects and, with full knowledge of their differences, classified them as belonging to a certain unit. So, Zeno considered dialectic a means of checking and of polemics while Plato considered it a means of determining the truth and, otherwise, a means of revealing the being in its true and permanently unchanging nature. "Τό ὄν καί τό ὄντως καί τό κατά ταὐτόν ἀεί πεφυκός ".(Philibus, 58 A).

For Plato philosophy was a deep experience. Influenced by Socrates' heroic death and by a life full of hardships and tribulations which led him from a rich aristocratic life to slavery, he came to acquire broad experience in life and the world. People's admiration was, in fact, what led him to philosophize in order to find Truth. In addition to this he was successful in all the sciences he applied himself to: mathematics, logic, geography, astronomy, psychology, etc.

Speusippus (447-339 B.C.)

Speusippus was Plato's nephew and succeeded his uncle in the Academy. Nothing is clear as regards his philosophical beliefs since his work Homea (Ὅμοια-Same Things) has been lost. It is said that even though Plato himself saw to Speusippus' education he was not without faults. In fact he expressed views which opposed those of Plato. In his Metaphysics (1072 B 30) Aristotle informs us that Speusippus, like the Pythagorians, contrary to Plato's beliefs, believed that Good does not exist as one from the beginning but results from or, rather, is achieved through an evolutionary process. "Ὑπολαμβάνουσιν οἱ Πυθαγόρειοι καί ὁ Σπεύσιππος τό κάλλιστον καί ἄριστον μή ἐν ἀρχῇ εἶναι ".(Ibid).Speusippus believed in the immortality of the soul and thought that happiness comes from living according to nature ("κατά φύσιν ζῆν"). At the same time he considered the world eternal and taught that pleasure is not good but considered riches and health beneficial.

We know that Speusippus developed the theory of "scientific sense" according to which the senses, inasmuch as they are guided by scientific method, can reveal to us the essence of objects perceptible through the senses. Conceptual objects can only be perceived by "scientific reasoning"-ἐπιστημονικός λόγος. Undoubtedly Speusippus had a Pythagorean inclination and this led him to found a philosophical science of numbers wherein numbers were taken to be the archetypes of beings. Speusippus also had a strong personality from which the skill for repartee was not lacking. This is evidenced by a conversation (in verse) he had with Diogenes the Cynic.

When Diogenes saw Speusippus, who suffered from rheumatism, being carried on a litter, he reviled him saying that it is not worth living in such a state. Speusippus answered him saying, "Man, Diogenes, does not live by his legs but by his mind ".

Xenocrates (394-314 B.C.)

Xenocrates succeeded Speusippus. Some people insist that he lacked "keenness of mind" without however, there being any proof of this. Quite the contrary, the fact that after Plato's death he went to Assus near Troy with Aristotle in order to establish a new Platonic school, combined with the fact that he, Speusippus and Aristotle took part in the great discussion on pleasure (hedone) which took place in the Academy bears witness to the fact that Xenocrates could not have been of mere average intelligence.

Xenocrates was the first to gather and personally publish Plato's work while he himself, being a voluminous writer, wrote a great number of books such as Logistica (9 volumes), Ta Peri Ta Mathemata (6 Volumes), Physikes Akroasis (6 books), Peri Diastematon, Ta Peri Astrologian (6 books) and many others. His last books alone numbered sixty, however almost nothing of these is extant.

As a person Xenocrates was ascetic and commanded great respect. His calm was legendary and his moral character led the Athenians to hold him in high esteem. Evidently he had studied the Pythagoreans, and more especially Philolaus, very well. Let us not forget that he had gone to Syracuse with Plato and Speusippus in order to hear them teach. Perhaps his study of the Pythagoreans explains his love of mathematics, which he considered so important that he did not accept a pupil in the Academy because he did not know any mathematics. He justified his rejection saying that the candidate did not have the background necessary for the study of philosophy "λαβάς οὐκ ἔχεις φιλοσοφίας ".

Xenocrates recognized three categories of knowledge: fame (δόξα), sensation (αἴσθησις) and understanding (νόησις). Fame may give a false impression or not. Sensation allows us to perceive the truth but not infallibly. Understanding gives us true knowledge. From another philosophical point of view, Xenocrates likened ideas to numbers and accepted the creation of all shapes and sizes from "indivisible lines" - " ἐξ ἀτόμων γραμμῶν ". This theory was opposed by Aristotle in his Peri Atomon Grammon (On Indivisible Lines). Xenocrates claimed that space is made up of indivisible lines meaning lines that cannot be divided.

According to Xenocrates the soul, which is considered a number which has substance, is self-propelled ("ἀριθμόν κινούντ' αὐτόν ἑαυτόν"), immortal and spiritual. It can exist outside the body as well. Moreover, he recognized the existence of goods of the body and goods of the soul giving priority to goods of the soul. Man's purpose is to fight to raise himself beyond the material element so that he might rid himself of his bodily bonds, something which can be accomplished by man's leading a virtuous life. However, leading a virtuous life means abstention not only from bad deeds but from bad thoughts as well. Typically, Xenocrates said that setting foot inside someone else's house is the same as casting a glance at it, "μηδέν διαφέρειν ἤ τούς πόδας ἤ τούς ὀφθαλμούς εἰς ἀλλοτρίαν οἰκίαν τιθέναι ". (Aelianus, Var. History, 14).

After Xenocrates the most famous members of the Academy whose beliefs have survived were: Crantor of Cilicia who originated consolatory speeches as a literary form with his Peri Penthous (On Mourning); Polemon, from whom the Stoic Zeno borrowed the famous "living according to nature" ("κατά φύσιν ζῆν"); Philippus, who published the Laws, the famous astronomer and mathematician Eudoxus; and Heraclides, who altered Democritus' theory on atoms to that of "unarticulated masses" that is, unconnected particles, and spoke of the earth's movement around its axis.

PERIPATETIC SCHOOL

ARISTOTLE

Aristotle (384-322 B.C.)

Aristotle was born in Stagira in Chalcidike. Still a young man, he went to Athens and became Plato's pupil. He studied under Plato for approximately twenty years. After Plato's death he went to Assus in Asia Minor as well as to Mytilene, where he taught very successfully. He was later engaged by Philip as a tutor to Alexander. Thus heroism and philosophy were combined. Greece benefited greatly from this combination since Aristotle, besides educating him, planted in Alexander's mind the idea of founding a world wide Greek State which Alexander later set out to create by means of his sword.

After living in Macedonia for six years as Alexander's tutor, Aristotle went back to Athens where he established his own school in the Lyceum (Lykeion/Λύκειον), the Peripatetic School. In the end, persecuted by the Athenians, he fled to Chalcis where he died of a stomach illness which had troubled him for years. Enough of his writings (which numbered over a for him to receive thousand) have survived for us to know his theories and unrivalled glory in the intellectual field.

Aristotle lived the political life practically and analyzed it scientifically with amazing clarity. First of all he accepted that man cannot exist alone. He must always be with others to whom he is connected by a blood relationship (phyle-"race", "tribe"). He creates political communities which exist by nature and not by argument/contention since man has an innate/inherent tendency to create communities with those to whom he is related by nature (homophyloi `of the same race).

"Κοινωνικόν ἄνθρωπος ζῶον πρός οὓς φύσει συγγένεια ἐστιν." (Eudemian Ethics- Ἠθικά Εὐδήμεια, 1942)

In his Politics Aristotle declared that man is a "political animal by nature." The purpose of the state is not only the safety of the citizens alone, but, more important, their achieving happiness (eudemonia) in a self-sufficient community. It is for this reason that the state ranks before the individuals and families which depend on it just as the parts of the body depend on the whole body."Τό γάρ ὅλον πρότερον ἀναγκαῖον εἶναι τοῦ μέρους ". (Politics 125, 3a) In this way Aristotle manifested his anti-individualistic views. Aristotle was, in any case, an adversary of all forms of democratic thought. This is evidenced by his belief that all men are not equal and so it is absolutely logical for people who are exclusively destined to be labourers to exist . These people are not fit to have civil rights and more so to rule others of the rest of the citizenry. In his Politics Aristotle approved of slavery without any false humanitarian sentiment. He maintained that the Greeks, being a superior race, and precisely because the excelled, were entitled to rule the others whom he collectively called barbarians.

We are all familiar with Aristotle's well known theory on forms of government. With the common good as his criterion, Aristotle distinguished three proper forms of government and three improper forms of government, which he called deviations. The proper forms of government are: monarchy (when one man governs for the benefit/good of the whole), aristocracy (when few govern for the good of the whole) and constitutional government (when many govern for the benefit of the whole). The improper forms of government, or deviations, are: tyranny (when one man governs for his own benefit), oligarchy (when few govern for their own benefit) and democracy (where many govern for their own benefit). The aforementioned distinctions as to forms of government, made by Aristotle, continue to be used in sociology and the science of government. They continue to sufficiently cover the topics: which form of government is proper , and why; and conversely, which is improper and why. All the forms of government which made their appearance after Aristotle's times can be placed into one of his categories. Aristotle, nevertheless, was not oriented toward any one system. For him any system which would be of benefit to the nation was acceptable as being proper. On the contrary, any system which would be harmful to the nation was rejected as being improper. The fact that Aristotle opposed and scorned democracy was never forgiven by the democrats who would surely have sentenced him to death if he had not managed to escape. He said that he would not allow a second showing of disrespect of philosophy (the first being Socrates' assassination.)

Regardless of the above, Aristotle favoured society's being governed by a select minority. He said that democracy might possibly be good if all citizens were good in virtue (arete) and other qualities. However, citizens are not equal and so democracy is harmful because it puts reality into order with an unnatural and non-existent equality as its basis. It is proper for those who excel, that is the elite, to rule and the people owe them obedience for they are the law. "Αὐτοί γάρ εἰσί νόμος" (Γ, η, 1).

In the area of ethics, Aristotle's statement that virtue (arete) is a mean and that it (virtue) finds and chooses the mean, has made a great impression. "Τήν δ' ἀρετήν τό μέσον καί εὑρίσκειν καί αἱρεῖσθαι...μεσότης ἐστιν ἡ ἀρετή." (Nicomachean Ethics, 1107 A). The mean Aristotle spoke of is not related to mediocrity but is rather placed between a lack and an excess. That is, if we take cowardice to be a lack and impudence as an excess then bravery is the mean and, at the same time, the virtue. Another example, taken from the table of the twelve moral virtues which Aristotle made up, is the case of generosity. Generosity as a virtue is the mean between avarice (a lack) and dissipation (an excess).

We must also note Aristotle's esteem for friendship, which he considered a virtue and a firm bond between cities."Τάς πόλεις συνέχειν ἡ φιλία ". (Ibid, 1155 A). In conclusion, Aristotle accepted Socrates' opinion as regards virtue (arete), this being that knowledge is necessary to the acquisition of virtue. Aristotle added, however, that exercise/practice (ἄσκησις) is also necessary. A Man's free will to choose, guided by his good sense, is a necessary condition for virtuous action. We need not discuss much further what virtue is since in his Nicomachean Ethics (1106 B) Aristotle says that it is a habit of the soul (ψυχική συνήθεια) which arises/ originates from the will which is kept at a mean defined by logic (ὁ λόγος) according to the definition which a wise man would give it. "Ἕξις προαιρετική, ἐν μεσότητι οὖσα τῇ πρός ἡμᾶς ὡρισμένη λόγῳ καί ὡς ἄν ὁ φρόνιμος ὁρίσειεν". Let us not forget that for Aristotle will meant a wish made after thought and which concerns things which are within our control. "Ἡ προαίρεσις ἄν εἴη βουλευτική ὄρεξις τῶν ἐφ' ἡμῖν ". (Ibid, 1113A).

Aristotle believed in enorasis, which is what we

today call intuition. It is through it without intervention of the intellect (διανοητικαῖς λειτουργίαις), that man can comprehend that which is true. Aristotle attributed the conception of axioms and general notions (γενικαῖς ἐννοίαις) used by scientists to enorasis. Bergson was to later reduplicate the theory on intuition.

Aristotle also contributed the terms potentiality (dynamei ontos, that which might possibly be) and actuality (energeia ontos, that which in fact is). The former symbolizes the fact that the possibility for development is inherent in potentiality; for example, the medical student happens to be a potential (dynamei) doctor, meaning that he might, under certain conditions, become a doctor. The latter describes in a way, the existing situation. That is, once the medical student has received his degree he is no longer considered a potential (dynamei) doctor but rather an actual (energeia) doctor. Related to the above terms is ἐνδελέχεια, which occurs when a being realizes all the existent and latent possibilities of development.

Other, equally important terms which Aristotle introduces into philosophy are generic terms. He also called genus (εἶδος) a form of matter. Genus means the active substantial core of beings to which they owe their unity and their capacity to act and react. Genus is not perceptible through the senses. It is energy, but there exists in the world not only genus, which is constant, but also another element to which Aristotle attributed the transiency which is manifest. There exists a second, passive, element upon which genus acts and gives it shape. Aristotle called this element hyle (ὕλη), taking the word from the language spoken at the time and which meant the timber (hylotomia) which is used in ship-building, furniture-making, etc. Just as timber takes on any shape, so the term hyle means exactly that; that it yields to any shaping which it is subjected to by the force of genus. Genus is superior to matter (hyle). Through it, or rather, through its action beings take shape and appear as they do in reality.

Theophrastus (372-287 B.C.)

Theophrastus, who came from Eresus of Lesbos, succeeded Aristotle as head of his School. According to Diogenes Laertius he was originally called Tyrtamus but was called Theophrastus by Aristotle because of his ability in the use of phrases. It seems that Aristotle esteemed not only his eloquence but also his excellence in philosophy and his honest character. Surely it was because of this great esteem that Aristotle bequeathed his library to Theophrastus in his will and left him as his son's guardian while also advising him to marry his daughter.

Theophrastus went to Athens at an early age. He became Plato's and then Aristotle's pupil. Theophrastus generally accepted Aristotle's theories and added certain details of his own, especially in the area of logic. Theophrastus stayed in Athens until his death, except for a short absence in about 318 B.C. during which time a law was passed forbidding, on penalty of death, the founding of a philosophical school without the permission of the Boule. Although he was friendly with Cassandrus of Macedonia and Ptolemy of Egypt, he remained in Athens where he had over 2.000 pupils and commanded great respect. He became very rich. Even though he was born of poor family, his father being a dyer, he had slaves and led a luxurious life. He maintained that the enjoyment of pleasures suits philosophers, as long as this is in moderation, because it allows them to rest and contributes to their happiness.

Theophrastus was a voluminous writer. He wrote about 250 books, some of which have survived whole as, for example, his <u>Peri Phyton Historia</u> (<u>Research Into</u>

Plants), and Peri Phyton Aetion (Causes of Plants) where he presented botany, phytogeography and plant physiology. Worthy of note is also the fact that the two aforementioned works were the only ones dealing with the study of plants even after the Middle Ages. His research into the colour of animals is also remarkable. He noted the relationship between the colour of animals and their environment, mentioned in the familiar theory of adaptation.

Theophrastus published equally important studies on the subject of religion. Even though he basically agreed with Aristotle, he did not hesitate to criticise many of his teacher's theories and to even question some of these as, for example, the purposeful action of nature, in other words, teleology, by citing as proof the fact that men have breasts without their serving a purpose. Also noteworthy is Theophrastus' theory on suppositional reasoning (ὑποθετική συλλογιστική) with which he supplemented Aristotle's logic.

Theophrastus is known to most people for his Characters in which he described thirty different characters with great pungency. This work was imitated by La Brugére (1645-1696) who published a treatise with the same title (Caractéres).

The Peripatetic School had other great philosophers as its members. Eudemus of Rhodes who, according to Simplicius, was the most genuine of Aristotle's associates ("γνησιότατος τῶν Ἀριστοτέλους ἑταίρων" In Physica 411) Aristoxenus of Tarentum who, in a treatise of his own which has survived, discussed the effect of music on man. Dicaearchus of Messene, who considered putting a way of life into practice, and not theories, of utmost importance. Demetrius of Phaleron who governed Athens for ten years but was later expelled by the populace who also destroyed the hundreds of bronze images they had made of him for his services to the country. Demetrius is considered the most voluminous writer of all the members of the Peripatetic School and was, in essence, the founder of the famous Library of Alexandria. Straton of Lampsacus who identified God with natural forces. Lykon of the Troad who was to remain a legendary figure well known for his wise advice and good humour. Ariston of Kea who wrote books on ethics. Critolaus who presented Greek philosophy to the Romans. Hermippus of Smyrna who was a biographer. Sotion of Alexandria about whom we do not have any information. The astronomer Aristarchus of Samos who discovered the solar system (ἡλιοκεντρικόν σύστημα) and who was a pupil of Straton. It seems that Straton also had great influence on the mathematician Archimedes. The astronomer Eratosthenes, the engineer Ctesibius/ Ktesibius , the physician Erasistratus as well as many other scientists were influenced by the Peripatetic School. For, the chief characteristic of the Peripatetic School was that it attracted, not masses of supporters, but rather distinguished scientists because of its scientific spirit.

STOIC SCHOOL

POSEIDONIUS

Zeno of Citium (334-264 B.C.)

Zeno, who came from Citium in Cyprus, got involved in philosophy by chance. Originally he had been a merchant but his ship sank and he lost all his property. In the end he found himself in Athens. Later, having perceived how important philosophy is for man, according to Diogenes Laertius (VII, 4) he said, "My trip went well because I was shipwrecked ". (" Νῦν εὐπλόηκα, ὅτε νεναυάγηκα"). Impoverished, he was reading Plato's Apology (of Socrates) one day when he remarked to a merchant friend, "People like Socrates don't exist any more ". At that moment, however, the Cynic Crates was passing and the merchant pointed him out to Zeno, saying. "Follow him ".

Zeno did indeed follow Crates and, influenced by him, wrote a book which he called Republic in which he expressed cosmopolitan views. It was said of this work that he wrote "on the dog's tail" meaning under Crate's guidance. Nevertheless, Zeno, who was not satisfied by the Cynic philosophy, turned to the Megareans and later followed the teaching of the Academic Xenocrates. However he was dissatisfied with the theories of the above philosophers and founded his own school which was called the Stoic School since the teaching took place in the Poikile Stoa.

We cannot say that he was a good orator; he nevertheless was a clever man of language, always creating new words. Although he was accused of copying the ideas of others, "τά δόγματα κλέπτων" (as the Academic Polemon claimed), he had a large number of pupils whom he greatly influenced. His exemplary life no doubt helped to make him successful. He was disinterested, frugal, dignified and moderate to such a degree that he was put forth as a measure of judgement so that when someone was to be praised for his self-control he was compared to Zeno, "τοῦ Ζήνωνος ἐγκρατέστερος ". His upright character was honoured by the Macedonian king, Antigonus Gonatas as well as by the city of Athens which crowned him with a gold wreath for his virtue and prudence.("Ἀρετῆς ἕνεκα καί σωφροσύνης ").

Zeno's death was proverbial. Once, in his old age, when he fell down, he called to the earth, "I am coming, why are you calling me?" ("Ἔρχομαι, τί μ' αὔεις; ") and then committed suicide by strangling himself. The Stoics accepted suicide as a moral principle. According to this principle life has no value when man, for reasons beyond his will - power, cannot achieve the happiness (eudaemonia) which serenity of the soul assures him of. When man is not able to give himself and others peace of mind, then life has no meaning and it is necessary to leave life by means of voluntary death. Thus, in a way, Zeno's ideal life was eudaemonism of the soul.

Zeno's writings, which were not few, have not survived. In any case, it may be inferred from what has been collected that he believed that scientific knowledge was a necessary condition for moral deeds. He distinguished three areas of philosophy, as did the members of the Academy: logic, physics and ethics. Zeno's contribution to philosophy and especially to ethics was very great. He laid the foundations for the meaning of duty. He, moreover, believed in a God who creates life, is the force which gives shape and motion to matter and supports beings. In the area of ethics Zeno maintained that man's logical nature is in a position to determine what is moral for him. Kant took this important aspect of the Stoic philosophy and based on it the ethical part of his philosophy in his Critique of Practical Reason. Besides the aforementioned view Kant borrowed one more equally important view from the Stoics. This is the view that God does not give man virtue (arete) but the good is attained after free choice. ("Ὁ θεός ἀρετήν μέν οὐ δίδωσι ἀνθρώποις, ἀλλά τό καλόν αὐθαίρετον ἐστι ")."Arete", according to Zeno, is something inseparable (ἀδιάσπαστον). Although there are many kinds of arete, arete is unique because all these kinds come from the basic arete which is prudence, good sense (φρόνησις). The four virtues (arete) which Plato distinguished that is good sense, bravery, common sense and justice, come from the basic arete. These four virtues are joined into one, "arete", and it is inconceivable that they should exist separately. It is necessary for all four virtues to exist together for "arete" to exist. In conclusion we must mention the moral precept of the Stoics, the famous "abstain and forbear" according to which man is led to happiness (eudaemonia) by means of abstention and endurance.

Zeno was succeeded by Cleanthes who, because of his physique, was called "the second Hercules". Cleanthes was so poor that he lived by working nights, drawing water from wells. He was so severe that he was observed reproaching himself whom he called an old man with white hair but without brains, "πρεσβύτη πολιάς μέν ἔχοντι, νοῦν δέ μή ". He wrote many works which are extant. In the end, he, too, committed suicide: by starving himself. Other important Stoics were: Sphaerus of the Bosporus* who taught Cleomenes the Spartan king; and also Persaeus of Citium* who was Antigonus Gonatas' teacher. Antigonus Gonatas later made him commander of his forces in Corinth where Persaeus fell in battle. Only the tittles of his works have survived, mentioned by various writers.

Chrysippus (281-208 B.C.)

Chrysippus came from Cilicia and made his first public appearances as an athlete: a runner. When he went to Athens he associated with the Stoics, more especially Cleanthes who left him as his successor as director of the Stoa when he died. He had also heard Zeno, the founder of Stoicism, teach. It seems, however, that Chrysippus surpassed Zeno in merit for it was said, "Without Chrysippus there would have been no Stoa". ("Εἰ μή ἂν Χρύσιππος οὐκ ἂν ἦν Στοά ").

By general admission, Chrysippus was an excellent orator and especially clever at finding dialectic arguments with which he confronted his opponents. At the same time he wrote over seven hundred tracts of which only a few fragments are extant. His works do not have the style and elegance of the writing of other philosophers because Chrysippus wrote quickly and did not pause to make corrections. As a person, he had rigorous principles and exemplary dignity. To honour these characteristics of his as well as his wisdom, the Athenians granted him civil rights (he was not entitled to them because he was not an Athenian) and, after his death (which is said to have been caused by strenuous laughter) his statue was created in the cemetery of Ceramicus.

Faithful to the principles of the Stoa, Chrysippus, too, proclaimed "unquestionably living according to Nature". ("Ὁμολογουμένως τῇ φύσει ζῆν "). In discussing the four virtues he maintained that bravery, common sense and justice are products of wisdom (σοφία). So, the wise man is virtuous and happy (eudaemon). Besides, the wise man is considered perfect. In fact nothing except insanity can take this perfection away from the wise man.

Chrysippus was a monist. That is, he believed that the primary substance of beings is one. Furthermore the world and all the beings were created by God, who is most good, most kind and most perfect since He was made of the most perfect material. God exists everywhere and the universes are to the world precisely that which the soul is to man's body. In the beginning God took a part of himself and created the world from it, going through a sequence of development. Air, water, earth and fire were created by the world's completion. The omnipresent soul of the world, which is God himself, rules over it (the world).

Politically, Chrysippus belonged to those who denied the equality of man and, consequently, democracy. His ideal was for one to become a wise man; in addition to this he accepted the supremacy of philosophers over the rest of the people who are totally ignorant. In fact he considers the masses foolish and so, insane according to the Stoic saying, "Πᾶς ἄφρων μαίνεται." ("Every unwise person is insane ").The masses are foolish and uneducated and so he did not care about what they said or did nor was it of any worth to him because it was said or done by the masses. He characteristically said, "If I paid attention to them I would not become a philosopher." ("Εἰ τοῖς πολλοῖς προσεῖχον, οὐκ ἄν ἐφιλοσόφησα ").

Perhaps the confiscation of his father's property was related to politics.(Diogenes Laertius, XI, 179). This opinion is supported by the fact that he accepted the civil rights granted to him by the Athenians without taking into account that his acceptance would degrade his home town. As likewise, in contrary to him, Zeno and Cleanthes had taken into consideration and had refused to accept the civil rights of Athens so as not to humiliate their home towns.

Just as all the Stoics, so Chrysippus believed that the soul is born as a tabula rasa whose content is composed of and enriched by objects. Chrysippus called this assimilation /representation (παράσταση) into the soul "heteroeosis" ἑτεροιώσις meaning change caused by them. Zeno and Cleanthes called "heteroeosis" "typosis" τύπωσις, meaning that the representation of beings was impressed into the soul.

Zeno of Tarsus and later Diogenes of Seleucia succeeded Chrysippus. Diogenes of Seleucia went to Rome where he gained the great admiration of his listeners. On orders from the Senate (Σύγκλητος) he returned to Greece together with Carneades and Critolaus with whom he had been sent as representative of Athens.

Poseidonius (135-51 B.C.)

Poseidonius, born in Apamea in Syria, is considered by general admittance, equal to Aristotle in knowledge and intelligence. For him philosophy is love of wisdom (sophia-σοφία) which, in turn, is defined as knowledge of divine and human affairs as well as of their causes. Poseidonius re-introduced a religious element into Stoicism by teaching, in addition, that we tend to the divine by means of virtue (arete). The soul comes from God and it finds itself on earth because it fell from the heavens because of a sin due to which it was sentenced to imprisonment in the body. Nevertheless, precisely because it comes from God, that is, it is part of the divine breath, it strives to return to its "lost Paradise." Great effort is required for the soul to reach the heavens through a life of virtue. This means that the soul goes through continual trials so as to become worthy of a return to the divine. This can be achieved only by those who manage to put aside desires of the body and keep the divine part of their hypostasis pure, free from corporal desires.

Poseidonius regarded the "know thyself" of the Delphic oracle as knowledge of the spiritual substance of the human soul as well as of that to which it is to return. Comprehension of the above will lead man to realize that he belongs to the "commonwealth of the Universe" (Πολιτεία τοῦ Σύμπαντος) to which all things, human and divine, belong. All the efforts made by science, civilization in general, and philosophy, more specifically, aim to re-establish man's connection with God. Consequently science, according to Poseidonius, has a moral destiny in that it contributes to man's perception of the world.

We can see that Poseidonius' work completes a religious and philosophical effort which starts from clear scientific knowledge and ends with the unexplored depths of a refined mysticism. This mysticism does not have a religious nature. We must not forget Poseidonius' belief that the Universe is divine (ἔνθεος), meaning that God's spirit gives everything life and soul. One of Poseidonius' most important assertions is that if we set sail from the furthest point west and have a constant easterly wind we will reach the Indies. This assertion was accepted by the Italian Tascanelli who worked out the maps with which Columbus set out for the Indies and in the end discovered America instead. Poseidonius' aforementioned assertion may be found in his Peri Oceanou where he furthermore explains the tidal phenomenon in relation to the moon and expounds interesting theories on the influence of climate on man's constitution. He elsewhere explains the appearance and development of religions with the same faculty of analysis. He maintains that in the beginning all men had one religion which came from the wonder the stars caused, the fear of the consequences of bad deeds, etc. Primitive people were closer to God than later generations which had religious customs etc. Prescribed by legislatiors who invested them with coercive force.

Of course we must not forget Poseidonius' theories that the cosmos is hierarchically made up of inorganic matter, planets, animals and man. Everything in them as well as relations between them is actuated by an order set by the wisdom of God. Nevertheless, there exist two worlds: the earthly one which is perishable/subject to decay and the heavenly one which is imperishable. The two worlds are connected by, or rather, to use Poseidonius' term are "linked" by, man who through his body participates in the decay of the earthly world and through his soul participates in the imperishability of the heavenly world. Thus the two worlds meet each other in man. There also exist other intelligent beings besides man. As he says in his Peri Heroon Kae Daemonon (On Heroes and Daemons) the air is full of such beings with which communication is possible. According to Poseidonius and Stoic philosophy the God about whom so much had been said had no form but could nevertheless take on any form. He wished to. God essentially is a fiery breath with the ability to understand. Poseidonius moreover believed in the power of divination and justified it on the strength of the "sympathy" which rules the universe in mutual relationships of parts of an organic whole. He made important observations about the moments when the bond between body and soul is relaxed, e.g. sleep, ecstasy, and when the soul can even perceive the future.

Poseidonius received many honours in Rhodes where he settled and lived. He was especially honoured by the Emperor Pompeius as well as the inhabitants of Rhodes, who sent him to Rome as their representative. Many Roman nobles became his pupils there. Prior to Poseidonius' stay in Rome, Cicero had visited him and had attended his lectures. The history of philosophy acknowledges his magnificent effort to make all the conclusions of the whole of Greek philosophy useful in a recapitulatory composition by putting them together.

Epictetus (50-120 A.D.)

Epictetus, too, belonged to the Stoic school of philosophy. We know very little about his life. While he was a slave, his master broke his leg and he remained lame ever since. Once freed he devoted himself entirely to philosophy. He lived in absolute accord with the teachings of the Stoa. Poor, with no home or family, in many respects destitute, he fought with amazing patience for the uplifting of man's morals (ἠθικοποίησις).

Epictetus was evidently an excellent orator. When the Emperor Domitian banished all philosophers from Rome, Epictetus went to Nicopolis in Epirus where he established his school. All who knew him were charmed by him and became his admirers and faithful friends. Typical of their great love is the following incident. After Epictetus' death one of his friends paid 3,000 drachmas to acquire the clay lamp that Epictetus had used.

Epictetus claimed that the fundamental problem in life is learning how to behave (φέρομαι) in life. His answer to the problem was that we should behave in such a way as to secure the serenity of our souls. We reach this peace only when we are not excited by passions, anxious to satisfy our appetites, and when we are to tormented by desires and generally not influenced by our opinions as to external matters.

Epictetus approved friendship, marriage and family but did not approve such a great attachment to them that, having these things, one is not moved by joy or losing them, one is crushed by sorrow. Throughout his teachings one finds a sense of destiny. He himself says, "Consider yourself the actor which the poet wants in [life's] drama. If the play is short, then be brief. If long then be long. If he wants you to play the part of a poor man, do so. If a lame man, a nobleman, a private citizen (ἰδιώτης), do so. For it is in your power to play well the role you were given, but it is someone else's power to choose the role you will play. (Epictetus, Enchiridion [Manual], XVII). A philosopher, Epictetus said, should keep away and remain indifferent to things which are not in his power. A certain indifference should prevail so that tranquillity of the soul will rule. As to his political beliefs, Epictetus taught that "every man has been created for something specific" (Ibid, XXVIII, 4) a fact which proves that he denied the abstract and general democratic equality of man. He was nevertheless animated by patriotic spirit. Besides he himself taught that it is one's duty and "reason" commands that you share danger together with your country. ("Ὁ λόγος ἐπιτάσσει νά συγκινδυνεύεις μέ τήν πατρίδα σου". Ibid , XXIX). As to the subject of God, Epictetus indisputably believed in His existence and taught that God rules all things well and justly. Epictetus called for man's voluntary submission to all the gods do. (Ibid). Addressing himself to man he frankly tells him that he is a piece of God and he has a part of Him in himself. "Σύ ἀπόσπασμα εἶ τοῦ Θεοῦ...ἔχεις τι ἐν σεαυτῷ μέρος ἐκείνου". (Treatises/ Discourses) (Diatribae).

Epictetus gave an interesting interpretation to the disputes which arise among people. He maintained that people have certain general beliefs which are the same for all people. He called these beliefs "prolepseis" ('preconceptions') "προλήψεις κοιναί πᾶσιν ἀνθρώποις εἰσίν". (Ibid , 22) For example, we all admit that that which is good is beneficial and preferable so that we should aspire to and search for it. All of us acknowledge that what is just is good and proper. Therefore no dispute arises as to the acknowledgement of common concepts which exist beforehand ("prolepseis"); however, opposition between people arises when they are to apply these "prolepseis" to the particular circumstances of external reality. "Ποτ' οὖν ἡ μάχη γίγνεται; περί τήν ἐφαρμογήν τῶν προλήψεων ταῖς ἐπί μέρους οὐσίαι". (Ibid.) For example, if one man says. "He did well. He is brave," and another replies, "He is not brave. He is mad," then a dispute inevitably arises due to the poor application of "prolepseis". In our example bravery and madness are "prolepseis". However, in this case we were led to a disagreement because the one considers the situation to be one of bravery (which everyone accepts as good) whereas the other considers it to be madness (which everyone accepts as evil). If the two men of our example had been able to apply "prolepseis" correctly, then they would not have disagreed but would have agreed that this someone was either brave or mad. The cause of people's wrong application of "prolepseis" lies in their wrong assessment of things (oeesis [οἴησις], `presumption', `arrogance'), which misleads them. Therefore the aim of philosophical education is to arrange "prolepseis" and to succeed in applying them correctly after clarifying which of these lie within our power and which not. Our bodies, relatives, property, country, etc. do not depend on us. On the other hand, our personalities depend on us as beings capable of choosing (voluntary ability-προαιρετική ἱκανότης) which deeds to perform and which not to. The correct use of this voluntary ability is, according to Epictetus, the Good which can be achieved through the strengthening of our souls, which can be educated to such a degree that what they desire is achieved."Οὐδέν ἐστιν εὐαγωγότερον τῆς ἀνθρωπίνης ψυχῆς. Θελῆσαι δεῖ καί γέγονεν ". (Ibid). So, man ought to look for and achieve the Good within himself."Παρά σαὐτοῦ λάμβανε ".(Ibid).

EPICURIAN SCHOOL

Epicurus (341-270 B.C.)

Epicurus was born in Samos. He occupied himself with philosophy from an early age. He observed the teachings of Pamphilus of the Academy and, finding himself on the island of Teon, he was later taught Democritus' theories by Nausiphones. After moving from place to place, he finally settled in Athens where he bought a garden and founded his own school. His pupils were originally called "those of the Garden". There were women and hetaerae in the garden and they all lived together in a community of friendship, philosophy and entertainment, a fact which gave rise to rumours that the Epicureans took part in orgies, etc.

Epicurus discussed the world, life and existence in approximately three hundred works of which only a few fragments have survived. Life's purpose, he said, is not what Plato or Aristotle said but rather the creation of a happy life (εὐδαίμων βίος). Philosophy is energy which offers us a happy life with thoughts and discussions. "Ἐνέργειαν λόγοις καί διαλογισμοῖς τόν εὐδαίμονα βίον περιποιοῦσαν ".Therefore the study of logic, for example, has merit only if it is directed toward happiness (eudaemonia). The same is true of the study of physics, which is useful only inasmuch as it contributes to the happy life ridding us of the fears and misconceptions created by our environment.

What is happiness (eudaemonia) thought ? According to Epicurus eudaemonia is pleasure (hedone), which pleasure is the beginning and end of the happy life. "Τήν ἡδονήν ἀρχήν καί τέλος λέγομεν εἶναι τάς τῆς ψυχῆς ". (Letter to Monoecus). Of course, there exist both spiritual and carnal pleasures. The spiritual ones are superior to the carnal ones. "Μείζονας ἡδονάς εἶναι τάς τῆς ψυχῆς". (Diog. Laert.); carnal pleasures, too, have their merit as do, for example, culinary concoctions, aphrodisia (sexual desire), music, works of art, etc. ("Χυλῶν ἡδονάς, ἀφροδισίων, ἀκροαμάτων, μορφῶν".) However, spiritual pleasures are superior to these because carnal pleasures last for only a short time whereas spiritual pleasures, chiefly through memory, remain in the soul for a long time.

Epicurus took care that harmful elements be eliminated from the meaning of pleasure so that his theory on pleasure would not be misinterpreted and wrongly explained. When he said pleasure, he maintained, he meant that this is the final aspiration of life and not the pleasure of prodigals who expend themselves in enjoyment as do some people who despise or are ignorant about or misapprehend his theories. When he said the word hedone (pleasure) he meant not suffering from bodily aches and not having a troubled soul. "Ὅταν οὖν λέγομεν ἡδονήν τέλος ὑπάρχειν, οὐ τάς τῶν ἀσώτων ἡδονάς καί τάς ἐν ἀπολαύσει κειμένας λέγομεν, ὥς τινες ἀγνοοῦντες καί οὐχ ὁμολογοῦντες ἤ κακῶς ἐνδεχόμενοι νομίζουσιν, ἀλλά τό μήτε ἀλγεῖν κατά σῶμα μήτε ταράττεσθαι κατά ψυχήν". (Diog. Laert. X) Indeed, Epicurus' position on the subject of pleasure is clear and is made even clearer with his assurance that he does not prefer all pleasure, without exception. "Οὐ πᾶσαν ἡδονήν αἱρούμεθα". (Ibid); he avoids those pleasures which cause them hardships which are greater than the pleasures enjoyed." Ἀλλ' ἔστιν ὅτε πολλάς ἡδονάς ὑπερβαίνομεν, ὅταν πλεῖον ἡμῖν τό δυσχερές ἐκ τούτων ἕπηται". (Ibid.)

On the other hand, he accepts certain pains when greater pleasure comes from them. The principle of all pleasure being good and all pain evil is applied on the condition that pleasure and pain will be examined and composed as to the pain or pleasure which follows them respectively. Then we will either accept or reject a pleasure or a pain, depending on the results of the comparison. In both cases it is beneficial for us to accept those circumstances in which pleasure prevails. Thus we accept a pain which leads to many pleasures or reject a pleasure which has many pains as a consequence. We are guided by our good sense in this choice.

As to his political beliefs, Epicurus was a genuine patriot, having served in the military and, as Diogenes Laertius says (X, 10) being unable to express his great love of country. "Τῆς πρός πατρίδα φιλίας ἄλεκτος ἡ διάθεσις". At the same time he was very devout. He believed that God is blessed and imperishable without troubling anyone and without being troubled by anyone; He is not affected by anger or pleasure for, if this were to happen, it would be an indication of imperfection."Πρῶτον μέν τόν Θεόν ζῶον ἄφθαρτον καί μακάριον νομίζων". (Letter to Menoeceus). Although he accepted the existence of God he denied all anthropomorphic conceptions of Him. Epicurus also recommended the performance of rites of worship as well as prayer, through which man approaches God. The Epicureans saw their ideal of bliss and freedom from troubles expressed in the personage of God.

Let us not forget Epicurus' moral beliefs on friendship. He taught that one should not abandon one's friends and, if need arise one should sacrifice one's life for them. "Καί ὑπέρ φίλου ποτέ τε θνήξεσθαι". (Diog. Laert. X, 120). It is stated elsewhere that whoever seeks his benefit incessantly cannot be a friend, but nor can a person who does not combine that which is beneficial with friendship. This is so because, in the first case, the good will which results from friendship is turned into a business transaction with good will paying for friendship and, in the second case, all hope for the future is cut off at its roots. "Οὔθ' ὁ τήν χρείαν ἐπιζητῶν διά παντός φίλου οὔθ' ὁ μηδέποτε συνάπτων. Ὁ μέν γάρ καπηλεύει τῇ χάριτι τήν ἀμοιβήν ὁ δέ ἀποκόπτει τήν περί τοῦ μέλλοντος εὐελπιστίαν". (Epicurus' Address - Ἐπικούρου Προσφώνησις, 39).

By far his most important contribution was Epicurus' explanation and establishment of sensationalism. He declared that thought depends on the senses to such a degree that nothing exists in man's intellect without having first existed in his senses. Moreover the senses are uncontrolled by the intellect inasmuch as thought depends on the senses. However, one sense cannot control the others since we obey all of them equally. Epicurus wrote a lot on the senses and all the sensationalists which came after him based their work on his. We cite the example of Marxism, which reproduced the Epicurean epistemology as such, and according to which knowledge is considered a reflection of independent objective reality.

Epicurus' death was very painful for it was caused by retention of the urine caused by kidney stones. "Τελευτῆσαι δι' αὐτόν λίθῳ τῶν οὔρων ἐπισχεθέντων". (Diog. Laert. X, 16). On his deathbed he asked his friends and supporters to remember his teachings "τῶν δογμάτων μεμνῆσθαι". (Ibid).

Among the important Epicureans were: Metrodorus of Lampsacus (Polyaenus' fellow citizen); Ermarchus of Mytilene, who wrote 22 books on the philosophy of Empedocles; Colotes, who polemically criticised Plato; Polystratus, who opposed the theories on the conventionalism of moral beliefs; Apollodorus, who wrote 400 books and who was called "Garden Tyrrant" (Κηποτύραννος) thanks to his behaviour; Zeno of Sidon who was Virgil's teacher; the physician Asclepiades of Proussa; Phaedrus, who taught Cicer who copied a book of his teacher's, On God, which he published with the same title; and many others about whom there is no information or whose books have been lost.

SCEPTIC SCHOOL

Pyrrho (365-270 B.C.)

Pyrrho was born in Elis and was the founder of the philosophical school known as "Skepsis" (Σκέψις). Pyrrho himself wrote nothing, but his beliefs, or rather, his doctrine was promulgated by his pupil Timon of Phlius who lived and taught in Athens. Pyrrho evidently was familiar with Protagoras' subjectivism which was, in a way, the forerunner of "Skepsis". We know that Pyrrho attended the Megarean School which was under the direction of Anaxarchus then. Pyrrho and Anaxarchus later took part in Alexander's campaign and reached the Indies.

Pyrrho maintained that all philosophical theories which seek the truth are wrong. Absolute truth and absolute falsehood do not exist. Therefore we should not be positive about those things which we believe in or deny but we should rather be cautious when we express opinions on things. In this way we will be able to enjoy the happiness which is achieved through the impassiveness and tranquillity of our souls.

Pyrrho declared that objective knowledge does not exist for we can trust neither our intellect nor our senses to infallibly ascertain the truth. Our senses are imperfect and present things as they seem and not as they are. In fact they often conflict in their determinations. For example, through the sense of sight we determine that a painting has projections and hollows whereas we determine through the sense of touch that neither exist. It is often true, or rather true as a rule, that people do not agree among themselves as to the nature of one thing or another. Thus, since our judgements on things are erroneous it would be best for us to avoid them or, in any case, doubt their validity.

So, the conclusions of the Pyrrhonic doctrine are that man cannot come to know the true nature of things and so it is not proper for him to voice opinions on them with assurance. "Τά μέν οὖν πράγματα ἀνεπίκριτα". (Eusebius, Proparaskeve Evangeliou - Εὐσέβιος, Προπαρασκευή Εὐαγγελίου [Preparation of the Gospel], 14) By extension, just as truth and falsehood do not exist, so justice and injustice, morality and immorality, etc. Do not exist. "Οὐδέν γάρ ἔφασκεν οὔτε καλόν οὔτε αἰσχρόν οὔτε δίκαιον οὔτε ἄδικον". (Diog. Laert. IX, 61). So, it follows that man's deeds are performed according to his subjective opinion and by custom because we cannot say, for each thing, that something is so and not otherwise. "Νόμῳ δέ καί ἔθει πάντα τούς ἀνθρώπους πράττειν οὐ γάρ μᾶλλον τόδε ἤ τόδε εἶναι ἕκαστον". (Ibid).

Because Pyrrho went to India it is believed that he came into contact with the gymnosophists there. However, a simple examination of Pyrrho's teachings proves the opposite. Pyrrho believed in indifference to all beings so as not to trouble ourselves whereas the Indian philosophers believed in annihilation. We must also make clear the fact that Pyrrho accepted the existence of external beings (ἐξωτερικά ὄντα-beings besides man) but maintained that these are not as our senses give us the impression they are. Οἷα γάρ φαίνεται τά πράγματα, μή τοιαῦτα εἶναι τῇ φύσει". (Ibid).

In proclaiming "incomprehension" (ἀκαταληψία), "reserve/restraint" (ἐποχή-suspension of judgement) and "speechlessness" (ἀφασία-not expressing opinions) the Sceptics reached "tranquillity" (ἀταραξία) which, as a state of the soul, assured them of happiness since all things that occur or happen to them are a common phenomenon and it is not worth one's while to suffer or, in any case, to be moved because of them. The Sceptics' password was "restrain yourself and say nothing ". ("Ἐπέχειν καί μηδέν λέγειν"). This peculiar refusal (ἄρνησις) of the Sceptics was both absolute and general, that is, it included them as well; for they did not define (ὁρίζω) anything so as not to contradict themselves. However, they did not say, "We do not define anything" ("οὐδέν ὁρίζομεν") for they would automatically define something even though negatively. They contented themselves with refuting the philosophical beliefs of the various schools.

Although Pyrrho had few pupils he was greatly honoured by the inhabitants of Elis. In fact, he was respected so much that he was named a high priest, which shows that he believed in God. Moreover, he must have felt a certain patriotism, having participated in Alexander's campaign. Pyrrho's pupil Timon was also an important Sceptic. In teaching that man cannot comprehend the true essence of things through either the senses or the intellect, Timon did nothing more than found the theory of "incomprehension" (ἀκαταληψία). In arguing against the belief that judgment, combined with the senses, can lead us to the Truth, he likened these two means of perception to two notorious swindlers of his time, wishing to stress how they deceive us in what they assert. According to Diogenes Laertius (IX) Timon would say, "Συνῆλθον Ἀτταγάς τε καί Νουμήνιος". Meaning that the two swindlers Attagas and Numinius had formed a partnership. The later European Sceptics reproduced the beliefs of the ancients.

Arcesilaus (315-241 B.C.)

Arcesilaus, who came from Pitane of Aeolis, wrote nothing and so we have come to know his beliefs indirectly. Originally, he was a pupil of Theophrastus but later had a close relationship with Pyrrho by whom he was influenced more. Arcesilaus started with Socrates' famous "I know only that I know nothing" to which he assigns the force of a general principle so that he even doubted the knowledge of our ignorance. He insisted that we should not give a definite opinion on anything and that we should practice "restraint" (ἐποχή) meaning we should avoid making judgements since Truth and Falsehood are indistinguishable. He cited the argument of the pile of grains of wheat. According to the argument three grains of wheat do not make a pile, nor do four grains etc., therefore a pile cannot be made by the addition of one grain of wheat, no matter how many grains are gathered. Or to present the reverse argument, if 20.000 grains make a pile of wheat if we remove the grains one by one we will still have a pile even if we reach the point of having but one grain. The fact that our senses and intellect mislead us led Arcesilaus to the belief that "restraint" (ἐποχή) is necessary in life.

Arcesilaus, nevertheless, denied the expression of opinion but not the performance of deeds, since action comes from the will and not from knowledge. Αἱ Παραστάσεις on which we must not express our opinions, arouse our will and stir us into action, which is right as long as this happens on the condition that that which is "reasonable" (eulogon) is its measure. Sextus Empiricus explains that which is "reasonable" as follows. He who practices "restraint" in all things will regulate all those things which he should prefer to do and all those things he should avoid doing according to that which is "reasonable". For happiness is perfected by good sense which acts in deeds which have been properly performed (achievements). A feat is that deed which, once done, can be acceptably defended. Therefore he who heeds what is "reasonable" will act properly and will be happy. "Ὁ περί πάντων ἐπέχων κανονιεῖ τάς αἱρέσεις καί τάς φυγάς τῷ εὐλόγῳ τήν μέν γάρ εὐδαιμονίαν περιγίγνεσθαι δια τῆς φρονήσεως, τήν δέ φρόνησιν κινεῖσθαι ἐν τοῖς κατορθώμασι, τό δέ κατόρθωμα εἶναι, ὅπερ πραχθέν, εὔλογον ἔχει τήν ἀπολογίαν· ὁ προσέχων οὖν τῷ εὐλόγῳ κατορθώσει καί εὐδαιμονήσει ". However the essence of that which is "reasonable" is not evident. We unfortunately have no evidence and can only speculate on the subject. However, the predominant opinion is that "reasonable" means that which most arguments tend to.

Other important Sceptics were Sextus Empiricus who wrote Outlines of Pyrrhonism (in three books) and Memoirs (11 books), which provide the basis of our knowledge about ancient Scepticism; another Sceptic was Aenisidemus of Knossos who wrote, among other books, Pyrrhoinioi Logoi (8 books).

PROBABILISTIC SCHOOL

Carneades (214-128 B.C.)

Carneades was born in the Greek town Cyrene in North Africa. In Athens he attended the Academy. He later became a director of the Academy and managed to once again give it sparkle. He himself wrote nothing; however we have come to know his theories through the writings of his pupils, chiefly of Clitomachus who succeeded him in the Academy.

Carneades caused a sensation in Rome where he and two other philosophers had gone as ambassadors. One day he spoke before a large audience and argued in favour of righteousness. The next day he argued against righteousness. He was enthusiastically applauded both times. However, the Senate, on Cato's urging, ordered him to leave Rome at once because it was considered that he endangered the established education of youths.

Carneades claimed that there are no criteria/is no way for us to ascertain the truth. Truth and Falsehood do, in fact, exist but man cannot distinguish the one from the other. The senses, thought and imagination deceive us. In fact one comes across meanings or images (dreams) which are false but which resemble true ones in all respects. Carneades called the absence of this contrast, or rather, difference between Truth and Falsehood "identity" (ἀπαραλλαξία). In his lectures in Rome he did nothing more than practically support his belief that for each thing or topic one can produce two arguments which are totally opposite but which are equally convincing.

Carneades' philosophical beliefs in a way have a personal tinge of opposition to Chrysippus whom he sarcastically called "Crypsippus" ("Horse-hidden") because his statue, due to size, was in a way, hidden by a horse nearby. Besides, not even he kept up appearances in his verbal attacks, often saying that if Chrysippus had not been a philosopher he would not have become one either. "Εἰ μή γάρ ἦν Χρύσιππος, οὐκ ἄν ἦν ἐγώ." Logical arguments are proven correct based on other premises which in turn are based on others until we reach unprovable axioms. No proof of their correctness, that is, of these correspondence with the truth, is presented.

Carneades criticized the beliefs of all the previous philosophical schools and especially the beliefs of the Stoics, which he refuted one by one. The Stoics claimed that God is virtuous. Carneades then argued: How is God virtuous? We cannot ascribe the virtue of bravery to Him for, in order for bravery to exist, there must be some danger to be faced so that who is brave and who is not will be evident. However, God does not face dangers, or let the Stoics at least tell us which dangers he faces. Carneades nevertheless believed in the existence of God who is not anthropomorphic, has no body, for he would then be subject to decay, nor soul, for he would then be subject to adulterating influence of impressions. For Carneades, God was absolutely inscrutable (ὑπερβατικός), inaccessible to human intelligence. It was thus that the mysticism which later flourished was born.

Carneades generally reacted against the Stoa's beliefs about God not because he wanted to claim that there is no God but because he wanted to prove that the Stoic's beliefs about God were wrong. Taken from the theoretical point of view, Carneades' method of subjecting all philosophical beliefs to philosophical examination allows us to call him the founder of <u>critical</u> philosophy.

Naturally the philosophers who preceded Carneades also examined and passed judgement on the ideas of their predecessors; however, none of the philosophers before Carneades had systematized criticism, or had made it the object of a whole field of philosophical activity as Carneades had done.

Besides critical philosophy, Carneades also established probabilism. Man is obliged to do something or, in any case, he is obliged to discuss a certain topic. Having acknowledged that definite knowledge does not exist, then what criteria is he to use to act on or think? Carneades declared that we should do or think that which we perceive to be or consider most probable. Thus, in the area of knowledge, probability takes the place of unattainable certainty. So probability, which has the following gradations is introduced into philosophy. The lowest degree is made up of images which we consider probable without their reliability being supported by the security of other images (likely fantasies). The next degree higher up is made up of images whose probability does not come into conflict with others or is not contested by others (likely, undisputed fantasies). The highest degree is made up of images which are examined from every aspect in detail and it is thereupon determined that there are no contradictions whatsoever with any images which are in any way related to them (likely, undisputed and limited fantasy). We must place Clitomachus in the probability school. He supported the view that "luck" is a prime factor in life.

ECLECTIC SCHOOL

Eclectism is a philosophical trend which seeks to gather elements which are apparently correct from various schools. It is mainly based on the belief that there are correct and erroneous beliefs in every philosophical system. Eclecticists propose that one choose and accept these theories which are correct.

Socrates himself said that he and his friends unfolded the written treasures of the ancient wise men and if they saw something good they picked it out. "Και τούς θησαυρούς τῶν πάλαι σοφῶν ἀνδρῶν, οὕς ἐκεῖνοι κατέλιπον ἐν βιβλίοις γράψαντες ἀνελίττων κοινῇ σύν τοῖς φίλοις διέρχομαι καί ἄν τι ὁρῶμεν ἀγαθόν ἐκλεγόμεθα." (Xenophon, Memoirs). Thus it is obvious that Socrates recognized the method of choosing certain views from philosophical theories one does not completely adopt. We certainly meet an eclectic comparison of views in almost all schools of philosophy; however, the eclectic school is that which does not present any other theory besides the systematic sorting of opinions from here and there, and putting them together in a kind of mosaic without their being in essence ombined to form a unique school.

Many factors contributed to the development of eclecticism, especially Scepticism which, through its deep, steady criticism, proved that no teaching is made up of sure beliefs. All teachings have weak points. This realization contributed greatly to weaken the rigidity of dogmas. Thus, the various schools were brought together by electicism.

Boethus of Sidon, for example, compounded Stoicism with Peripatetic philosophy on the subject of divinity which he thought existed in the air (Stoa) but also distinguished it from the cosmos (Aristotle). After Boethus came many philosophers who accepted other schools' ideas into their systems, or at least modified their inflexibility. For example, Philo of Larisa sought something between Carneades' probability and the Stoics' sure knowledge. Antiochus Ascalonites, who taught Cicero was also an eclecticist. He attempted to prove that the philosophers of the Peripatetic School, the Academy and the Stoa differed in unimportant matters. It is generally accepted as a fact that Potamon of Alexandria gave his school the name "eclectic". He systematically gathered those elements which pleased him most from each sect, as Diogenes Laertius says. We will give mere details on Panaetius of Rhodes for the sake of history. He distinguished himself in eclectism and so detached himself from the dogmation of the Stoa.

Panaetius (180-99 B.C.)

Panaetius of Rhodes was a remarkable person who made the Greek spirit shine throughout the world once again. After studying in Athens and Pergamum he went to Rome where he associated with Scipio Africanus to whom he was an advisor. Panaetius evidently met the reknown historian Polybius in Rome. Polybius was, at that point, a political captive. An admirer of Plato Panaetius called him "The Homer of philosophers" and, thanks to Platonic ideas, abandoned many of the beliefs of the Stoic school which he belonged to as head of the Stoa.

For Panaetius the world is born and so not subject to decay. The soul is not immortal but, being made from a mixture of air and fire, it dissolves after death. Thanks to the existence of fire it comes into contact with universal reason (λόγος). At the same time, thanks to the existence of air, it comes into contact with nature, which is irrational. Thus, according to Panaetius, the soul comprises its logical part, called "hegemonical", on the one hand, and on the other hand, its irrational part called "nature" (physis). The hegemonical portion is that which can and ought to govern nature. The distinction between that which is rational and irrational in man had, no doubt, already been made by Plato, who believed the soul to be spiritual and immortal. "Ψυχή πᾶσα ἀθάνατος" (Phaedrus, 254C), and Aristotle, who recognized immortality in the intellectual strength of the soul.(De Anima,430A)

As to religious matters, Panaetius accepted the existence of God, insuring the order and harmony of all things without, however, intervenening in the lives of men thereafter. Although a Stoic, he rejected the Stoics temperance. Man should guide his irrational nature by means of the strength of his reason. It is not proper for man's passions to be canceled for they were given man by Nature; however, these passions ought to obey the rules and conform to the guidelines set by logic. Therefore the moral ideal is not Stoic "apathy" (the eradication of passions) which results from inaction, but rather the satisfaction of the soul which is attained when man does good deeds. This satisfaction was called "euthymia" (good humour).

Politically Panaetius denied the equality of man since he believed that each man has his own individuality which is different from the individuality of others. These views are presented under the guise of individual predispositions. Cultivating these predispositions if they are good is one of the purposes of education. The existence of an individual nature in man undoubtedly disproves the democratic idea which maintains that men are equal among themselves.

Panaetius, being descended from a military family had, moreover, a strong sense of the fatherland (patris). Due to his belief that one's native town (patris) is always closer to one even if one enjoys more honours in another town, Panaetius refused to become an Athenian citizen saying that one patris is enough for a wise man. "Οὕτω δέ καί τήν οἰκείαν πόλιν ἐγγυτέραν τῆς μή οἰκείας κἄν μᾶλλον τις ἐν ταύτη τυγχάνει τιμώμενος διά τήν κατά φύσιν σχέσιν. Καί ὀρθῶς ὁ Παναίτιος, πολίτην αὐτόν ᾿Αθηναίων ποιεῖσθαι σπευδόντων, εἶπεν, τῷ σώφρονι μίαν πόλιν ἀρκεῖν ".(Plutarch, ... to Hesiod, 65). Imbued with such national sentiment, Panaetius, as well as Polybius, finding themselves in Rome and using Scipio's friendship, managed to help their country. "Τῇ Σκιπίωνος εὐνοίᾳ πρός αὐτούς μεγάλα τάς πατρίδας ὠφελήσαντες". (Plutarch, Moralia, 814 B').

One of Panaetius greatest contributions to mankind was his introduction of humanism to Rome and thence to the West. Panaetius' humanism (ἀνθρωπισμός) consisted of a combination of that which is "good" and that which is "proper", which was opposed to the "that which is `beneficial'" of materialism. He expressed his moral beliefs as well as his theoretical effort for the betterment of society in a number of works. One of his works, Peri Kathekonton (On what is appropriate), was duplicated by Cicero who called his work De officiis thus copying not only the content but the title as well. For Panaetius the moral ideal was living according to that which Nature places at our disposal: "τό ζῆν κατά τάς δεδομένας ἡμῖν τῆς φύσεως ἀφορμάς τέλος ἀπηφήνατο ". (Clement, Stromateis(Στρωματεῖς), 2, 129). In conclusion let us not forget that Panaetius also discussed the relationship between people and the geographical location of the country they live in.

NEO-PLATONIC SCHOOL

Ammonius Sakkas (3rd cent A.D.)

Porphyrius/Porphyry says that Sakkas' parents were Christians but even though raised as a Christian Ammonius espoused the national religion. (He is said to have been called Sakkas [from the word "sack"] because he worked as a porter). He died in 242 A.D. without leaving any writings. We therefore do not know exactly what the founder of the Neo-Platonic school taught and to what degree he influenced his pupil Plotimus. Great disagreements as to the reliability of a variety of information about Sakkas have arisen among German researchers. Zeller, Arnheim and Heinemann attempted to provide evidence to prove or disprove the reliability of the passages in the books by Nemesius and Hierocleus which refer to Sakkas' beliefs. His pupils' beliefs, nevertheless, help us form an idea about what Sakkas believed.

Among Sakkas' pupils were: Plotinus, whom we will discuss further on, Origenes (or Origen) (not the ecclesiastical writer, who had heard him teach), who wrote two books, On Daemons (Peri Daemonon) and " Ὅτι μόνος ποιητής ὁ Βασιλεύς " wherein he expounded on the belief that there exists one God, the creator above all and Erennius, who made Sakkas' teaching known publicly thus breaking the agreement not to reveal any of Ammonius' teachings ("μηδέν ἐκαλύπτειν τῶν Ἀμμωνίου δογμάτων"). About 1600 the Polish national hero, Zamoiski, financed Sinionides' publication of Erennius' books entitled Exegesis to Metaphysics. In this work one finds all the arguments used by St. Augustine against the theories of the Sceptics as he presented them in his book On the Trinity (10). Also among Sakkas' pupils were Longinus, who distinguished himself as a scholar and was put to death by the emperor Aurelius; Amelius, and many others about whom we have no information.

Plotinus (205-270 A.D.)

Plotinus is the most reknown representative of that philosophy which is known as Neo-Platonism. He was not young when he turned to philosophy without having definite views and constantly changing his affiliation to philosophical schools until he met Ammonius Sakkas. After his teacher's death he took advantage of the Roman campaign and went to Persia. After that he went to Antioch and thence to Rome where, now a well-rounded philosopher, he taught and amazed the people there. The créme de la créme of the Roman aristocracy followed his teachings. Among them was the Emperor Gallienus whose wife considered Plotinus sent from God.

Plotinus' pupils literally adored Plato and, of course Socrates, in whose honour they had special holidays with all possible formality. His pupils had such great respect for Plato and Socrates that, on Plotinus' suggestion, Gallienus intended to found a city in Campania which was to be called Platonopolis and where Plato's principles on the State (Republic) would be applied. Adverse circumstances, however, such as the Emperor's death and Plotinus' blindness, upset these plans.

The beginning of Plotinus' philosophy is God and its end is union with God. God is a ὑπερβατικόν being which is inaccessible to the mind (nous). He is everywhere and the universe and all forms of life were made of-by Him. Man can conceive of Him only in terms of experience, mystical vision and theory. It is from God, who is incorporeal, that beings were born and it is to Him that they will go in the end. We move within this necessity. As human beings we partake of the earthly and divine worlds between which there is an irreconcilable opposition. This opposition upsets the soul for it seeks a position in favour of that which is sensible or insensible (unable to be perceived by the senses). The soulbeing predestined to reach the insensible world, is obliged to struggle against the sensible world.

God, who is indefinable, does not have properties/ qualities and is symbolized by the "Absolute One" for Plotinus. This One in a way produces all things by means of radiation. In other words, the One overflows because of its superabundance and beings are formed from its emanation. The creation of the world is therefore not a voluntary act of God but rather a necessary afflux which nevertheless does not reduce Him. The first thing to emanate is the mind (nous), which is the supreme being and consists of ideas which are the perpetual archetypes of beings. Then the divine force creates the cosmic soul which in turn gives rise to a second soul called nature (physis) according to Plotinus and which is connected with the body of the world much the same as the human soul is connected to the human body. The cosmic soul gives birth to other souls which, depending on their origin, scatter and go to the different parts of the world and bring the insensible world close to the sensible world. If we descend further then we reach matter. So, the world beyond our senses consists of the One, the Mind and the Cosmic Soul.

Then comes the world of the senses, which is material and is the expression and cause of evil. The Soul fell to the earthly world and in order to return to the world beyond the senses it must detach itself from matter and all corporal things. This detachment is called catharsis and can be achieved without the Stoics' temperance which Plotinus nevertheless indulged in.

The final purpose of philosophy is viewing the One. Naturally the intellect has its own value however it cannot help us in this case because the area of the One is beyond the intellect. We reach that area of knowledge by means of a mystical vision. Thus a kind of religious mysticism is founded. Our soul becomes one with the Divinity even though it participates in the earthly life. It is possible for the soul to be freed from/of the bonds of matter and so be elevated to the insensible world by means of love, art and philosophy.

The purpose of the moral life as may be inferred from the above is to rank with God. "Θεῷ ὁμοιωθῆναι" (Enneads 1,2). The first step towards this ranking is a flight from the sensible world which is initially achieved with the attainment of virtue. Catharsis is the next stop and finally, through "heavenly eros" and ecstasy man completes his difficult climb upward.

Plotinus' works were published by his pupil Porphyry under the general title of Enneads. In fact, Porphyry attempted to popularize Plotinus and wrote many works against Christianity to this end. However, the Emperor Theodosius II had them burned.

SYRIAN SCHOOL

Iamblichus (270-330 A.D.)

Iamblichus was born in Chalcis Syria. He was admired by the Emperor Julian; however, we do not have much reliable information about him. It seems that he was greatly respected by his pupils who called him "divine". It is a known fact that his philosophical beliefs are of a theological nature to such a degree, in fact, that he accepted the existence of "sacerdotal" virtue by means of which man reached the primordial being.

A number of Iamblichus' works are extant and these give us ample information about his ideas. His ethics is developed under the influence of his religious tendencies. In his book On the mysteries (Peri mysterion) he explains that man will succeed in rising to the Primordial Being. He also believed in Fate, which is all-powerful and determines man's life. Man can never rid himself of Fate unless the gods, who are the only ones worthy of conquering Her (Fate), help him.

Iamblichus was undoubtedly influenced by Plotinus and Porphyry; it is said that Porphyry was Iamblichus' teacher when the latter found himself in Rome for a while. Iamblichus nevertheless presented his own ideas through which he attempted, in a way, to bring the Greek gods into accord with the other gods. His ultimate goal was to present a complete religio-philosophical system with which he could fight against Christianity.

Plotinus spoke of the One as the first principle of beings. Iamblichus, however, placed the so-called "ineffable principle" above it/the One. This "ineffable principle" gives rise to the One which is the Good followed by the mind (νοῦς) divided into the spiritual part (souls) and the intelligible- νοητόν part (ideas). The spiritual part is in turn divided into mind (νοῦς), strength (dynamis), and creator (demiourgos); the intelligible (νοητόν) part is divided into existence, force of existence and understanding of force. After these distinctions we have new subdivisions in threes where the worldly and supra-worldly gods belong and then many more divisions by three. In the end we reach the angels, the daemons and the heroes. Iamblichus showed originality in religious matters. Despite accusations ascribing fanciful thinking to him he was absolutely logical in his logical analysis, as is proven by his writings in the field of mathematics. He was wrongfully accused of turning the source of philosophy (critical doubt) into "caricature". This may have been so because he believed that miracles have a logical basis (accepted by modern science). Or, because he believed in divine revelation as a means of contact with God. Or, because he believed that priests, expressing the divine revelation, are superior to philosophers.

It was Iamblichus who first introduced the dialectic which proceeds in triads into philosophical thought. This dialectic was reproduced by the German idealist Hegel who was, in turn, imitated by Marx. Iamblichus taught the triadic cycle of development as follows: There exists that which remains, "the remainder" (τό μένον). Then comes that which emerges, "the neon" ("new thing"), and lastly that which causes reversion, "the epistrephon" ("one returning"). In other words, Iamblichus believed that in each triad, which comprises a complete system ("arrangement"-διάκοσμον) there is a primary element (Hegel's "thesis"), a resulting element which is the opposite of the first (Hegel's "antithesis") and the third element which creates a compound result from the first and second elements (Hegel's "synthesis"). Iamblichus also supported the view that the world is eternal and that man lies between superior and inferior beings. He by no means accepted the belief that man's soul is reincarnated after death in the bodies of animals because animals lack reason. Among Iamblichus' most reknown pupils were Sopatrus , who was put to death by Constantine I, and Aedesius, who became the director of the school.

PERGAMUM SCHOOL

Aedesius (4th cent. A.D.)

Aedesius, who was Iamblichus' pupil, went to Pergamum where he found his own school. He stirred up the interest of the educated citizenry among whom were the Emperor Julian's teachers, Eusebius and Chrysanthius, and the Emperor himself, who turned against Christianity. Aedesius' works are not extant nor do we have more information about him, a man who was acknowledged to be outstanding by his contemporaries.

ATHENIAN SCHOOL

Proclus (410-485 A.D.)

Proclus was born in Constantinople. He was one of the most famous representatives of the ancient Greek spirit. In Menandria he studied mathematics and philosophy, devoting himself especially to the study of Plato and Aristotle. He later went to Athens where he attended a number of lectures by Plutarch the Athenian. When he took over as head of the Academy he was very successful in spreading his ideas. His impressive and dignified appearance as well as his virtuous and exemplary life helped him impose his ideas. He was persecuted by the Christians and forced to remain for a while in Asia where he had fled to.

Proclus' beliefs were undoubtedly influenced by the teachings of the Pythagoreans whom he held in great respect. The Pythagoreans' mysticism evidently left a religious stamp on Proclus' philosophy which had/was of a θεουργικός nature/character. For Proclus, religion and philosophy are merely two roads that led to the truth, the difference being that the former uses symbols where the latter uses ideas. God is absolutely ὑπερβατικός transcendental . It is for this reason that the human mind cannot conceive of him. The first principle of beings, called "τό αὐτό ἕν", that is "the true one" is inaccessible to the human mind. It is from the first that the "nines" emanate, or rather, are produced by triads/threes. These "nines" (enades) are complete beings which lie beyond the senses. Then, through development (which is completed by a return to the "one), by triads once again, the mind (nous) is created. The mind by a new development by triads in reality presents/reveals "that which is comprehensible" (νοητός) with the quality of matter, "that which is both comprehensible and spiritual" (νοητός καί νοερός) with life being its quality, and "that which is spiritual" (νοερός) with the intellect being its quality.

We see that Proclus accepted and adapted Iamblichus theory on development by triads. According to this theory all beings are produced from a first principle, a "cause without cause", by means of a ceaseless triadic development. The following are the stages of development. The first constitutes the primary substance, which remains itself (single). The second comes from the fact that something which is created from the primary substance is different from it thus giving rise to a type of progress (progress) and the third stage is completed by virtue of that quality of progress by which it is related to the primary substance from which it was produced. Progress both resembles (because it had its origins in it) and differs from (because it departed from it) the primary substance. Thanks to its similarity it is related to and seeks to join itself to the primary substance (return).

Each triad is further divisible into other triads which are further divisible into other triads, and so on. Proclus gave these triads names of Greek gods. According to Proclus the soul is made up of a rational and irrational element and, moreover, a divine force thanks to which man manages to communicate with the gods. Only by leading a virtuous life can man reach the gods. On its way up the soul passes, in turn, the stages of eros, truth, and faith. At the end of its ascent the soul will be in a position to see the exemplary models which exist in the mind of the divinity, that is the archetypical ideas: "θεώμενος τά ἐν τῷ θείῳ νῷ παραδείγματα." Proclus had reached this state. His biographer, Marinus, states this in his work Proclus (22) from which the above citation was taken.

During the period we are now describing there was a widespread effort to protect the national religions from the spread of Christianity. Proclus and other philosophers participated in an effort to protect the ancient religions. They presented theologies which were able to oppose the new faith. In fact, many philosophers became priests and organized ceremonies whose rituals were suited to religion. Moreover, there was an unusual competition concerning the performance of miracles between Christians and Nationalists. Marinus (who was a mathematician) notes that once, when Proclus was seriously ill, a young handsome lad appeared above his bed, laid his hand on the ill man's head, cured him at once and disappeared "καί τῆς κεφαλῆς ἐφαψάμενος, ὑγιῆ ἐξαίφνος ἐκ κάμνοντος ἀπετέλεσε καί οὕτως ἀφανής αὐτῷ ἐγένετο" (Proclus, 7). Proclus' death was likewise veiled in mystery. On that occasion a deep darkness fell and the stars disappeared: "σκότος γάρ ἐγένετο βαθύ καί ἀστέρες ὤφθησαν ". (Ibid.)

It is a well-known fact that Proclus, who gave his entire property to charity, was held in great esteem by both the educated populace and the masses. In the end the quarrel between the Christians and the Nationalists was ended, not by common agreement, but by a decree issued by Justinian in 529 A.D. This decree closed down the schools of philosophy and forbade its teaching, "πρόσταξιν ἔπεμψεν, ἐν ᾿Αθήναις κελεύσας μηδένα διδάσκειν φιλοσοφίας," as the chronicler, John Malalas, says.

Damascius (458-535 A.D.)

Damascius was born in Damascus. He studied philosophy and astronomy in Alexandria. Then he went to Athens where he became Marinus' pupil and later succeeded him as head of the school. After studying the subject of evolution from the first principle as presented by Iamblichus, whom he greatly respected, he concluded that it is impossible for the superior being to produce an inferior being. Therefore there is only one single indivisible-ἀδιάκριτος- being. He wrote many works among which the most important were Questions and Answers on First Principles and On Number, Place and Time.

Justinian forbade the school's works and seized all its property. Enraged by this coercion, Damascius and his followers departed for Persia where they settled in the court of King Chosroes. They left almost immediately, however, because they could not bear the lack of intellectuality which existed there. The others returned to Greece but Damascius disappeared from that point on. It is a noteworthy fact that Simplicius, who is one of the best commentators on Aristotle's works, was Damascius' pupil. There were two other important representatives of the Athenian School: Marinus, Proclus' successor and biographer, who interpreted Plato; and Isidorus who criticised his times and presented the "heroic period" as a model.

ALEXANDRIAN ERA

HYPATIA

Hypatia (4th cent. A.D.)

Hypatia was the daughter of the famous Greek mathematician Theon . She, too, applied herself to mathematics and astronomy. She was so good in geometry that she was called "geometer". The practical sciences, as well as research into these sciences prevailed in the Alexandrian School. This was preferred to the vague study of metaphysical things. Thus Aristotle's logic was of primary importance, without this meaning that Plato was ignored. The school was well-known for its religious tolerance. This made it an educational establishment παιδευτήριον for all those who were interested in philosophical matters, regardless of their religious beliefs. It is considered that, in this respect, the school contributed a great deal to the smooth transfer of the ancient Greek sciences to the Greco-Christian Empire of Byzantium.

After studying in Alexandria, Hypatia went to Athens and studied at Proclus' Athenian School. On her return to Alexandria, she began teaching Neo-Platonism while also presenting the works of Aristotle and other famous Greek thinkers. Hypatia also taught mathematics and astronomy, subjects on which she also wrote books as, for example, Astronomical Canon. Combining theory and practice, she devised the astrolabe (an instrument used to determine the distance of the stars from the horizon) which her pupil Synesius, who was later to become Bishop of Ptolemais, constructed.

Historians agree that Hypatia was, in a way, a phenomenon in the history of philosophy for there were no women philosophers before her nor after her. She was extremely beautiful, as well as intelligent and versatile. All historians have sung the praises of her remarkable combination of beauty and wisdom. Fate held a tragic end in store for her. In 415 A.D. a crowd of Christians, incited by Cyrillus, Bishop of Alexandria, seized her, tore her clothing and, after leaving her naked, cut her into pieces with seashells and burned her pieces: "ἀποδύσαντες τε τήν ἐσθῆτα ὀστράκοις ἀνεῖλον καί μεληδόν διασπάσαντες ἐπί τόν καλούμενον Κυναρεῶνα τά μέλη συνάραντες πυρί κατηνάλωσαν."

Synesius (370-413 A.D.)

Synesius came from Greece. He was a pupil and admirer of Hypatia whom he called "most divine". An excellent orator and shrewd politician, he succeeded in defending the interests of his home town when he was sent to Constantinople as an ambassador. He wrote many noteworthy scientific works as well as ten hymns in the Doric language which are also worth of note. He had a great love for Greek culture and had a deep knowledge of Greek philosophy. He soon realized what political significance for Greece the spread and prevalence of Christianity had. Thus Synesius espoused Christianity and became Bishop of Ptolemais. He nevertheless placed one's country, which he called "living mother" ("ἔμψυχος μητέρα") (1336, Vol. 66, Migae), above all else. He proclaimed that a philosopher is always patriotic (Ibid., 1493) and willing to sacrifice himself for his country (Ibid., 1496).

In the area of philosophy, Synesius worked towards a combination of Neo-Platonism and Christianity. He finally presented a form of Christian humanism, at least as acknowledged by the German scholars of ancient Greek philosophy (Zeller, et. al.) His correspondence with Hypatia is of great scientific and historical importance. Fortunately this correspondence was not completely lost.